**Praise for** *Master the Intervi*

By the time you have an interview for a job you really want, the stakes are high. You are SO close. You don't want to blow it. Ideally, you want to wow them. Yet most professionals are not great at interviews. To be honest, most are terrible, and this includes people who graduated from Harvard Business School and similar places. Why? Because they don't have a game plan and they haven't put in the work required to execute a good one. So they get close to their dream job or even just an okay job, and they don't get it.

The basic premise of *Master the Interview* is that you don't have to be that person. In this comprehensive book, Anne Marie Segal, a coach, lawyer and writer's writer, sets forth ALL the relevant aspects of interviewing effectively so that you can anticipate them, prepare for them and ultimately master them and get the job you want. These include identifying competencies, communicating value, having good questions to ask, talking about interests, and the complex etiquette of managing social cues, and many more. She does a particularly good job of specifying situations and explaining why one type of statement is going to help you and another type will hurt you.

It's about time that someone took the time to go DEEP into the mechanics of effective interviewing. You can either study the whole book or identify the parts you need. Either way, it's worth your money and even more, it's worth your time.

- Michael F. Melcher, Executive Coach and Author of *The Creative Lawyer: A Practical Guide to Authentic Career Satisfaction*

It's a really terrific and practical book that helps people think about themselves in an organized and disciplined way while prepping for an interview.

- Lisa Maguire, Financial Services Professional

Segal's debut work is divided into five parts, each addressing a different aspect of the interview process. [It's] all packaged in a helpful way, effectively integrating open-ended questions and self-assessment exercises into each chapter. This is probably the strongest aspect of the book, as these queries immediately immerse job-seekers in the interview process so that the event itself will seem less formidable.

A self-directed, interactive manual that should benefit experienced and new job-seekers alike.

- *Kirkus Reviews*

# MASTER THE INTERVIEW:

# A GUIDE FOR WORKING PROFESSIONALS

Anne Marie Segal

The author has been very careful to provide accurate information in this workbook, but errors and omissions may occur. Please consider this possibility when making any important decisions about interviews or your career.

*****

**Cover photograph:**

Rob Marmion/Shutterstock.com

**Author photograph:**

ISBN 978-1-53916-516-3

To my husband, Mario Segal,
who cheerfully endured my creative process, including untold evenings of
"just finishing up this one sentence, I'll be right there…"

and to my children, Daniel and Tamara,
my favorite and greatest cheerleaders and advisors

# ACKNOWLEDGEMENTS

There are many people without whom this book would not have been possible.

I thank my clients, colleagues, friends and others for generously sharing with me what they are experiencing in a range of interview settings and helping me lay the groundwork for many of the points I discuss here. I also acknowledge and thank the many professionals and students who have attended my presentations on career topics and asked insightful questions or shared comments about their own interview experiences.

I appreciate the early readers who have given me support during this time of intense writing and editing, as well as those individuals who have graciously provided comments on drafts or quotes in this book, some of whom prefer to remain anonymous. Their input was invaluable at many stages of the writing process. Michelle Jonjak (who truly went above and beyond), Mark Stromberg, Amanda Sherman, Charles Moré and Gary Jacobi deserve special mention here.

At the same time, I have benefitted from my membership in the National Résumé Writers' Association (NRWA) and participation in its recent conference in Annapolis. I treasure the relationships with new and existing friends and colleagues who joined me there and thank the NRWA's fabulous board members, conference organizers and presenters. It is truly a collaborative group.

Finally, I thank my parents, husband and children, as well as my nanny Silvia Garcia. In particular, I am blessed to have a family who believes in me, made time for this project in our busy schedules, provided helpful feedback as I discussed portions of the book at length (or, in the case of my children, who at ages 12 and 10 think this topic is very boring, offered cover design suggestions and marketing ideas!) and gave me the opportunity to write.

# TABLE OF CONTENTS

# PART 2: YOUR VALUE PROPOSITION

# PART 3: INTERVIEW QUESTIONS

**CHAPTER 10**

# PART 4: UNWRITTEN RULES OF INTERVIEWING

**CHAPTER 11**

# FOLLOW-UP ON TOPICS IN THIS BOOK

For additional copies of the workbook portions in this book, please visit my blog at www.annemariesegal.com and click on "Worksheets."

If you have any further questions about the topics or information presented here, please contact me at:

Anne Marie Segal
**SEGAL COACHING**
Stamford, CT

email:    asegal@segalcoaching.com
website:  www.segalcoaching.com

I receive many emails and other requests each day, and I endeavor to respond to each inquiry within 24-48 hours, if not sooner.

Separately, if you have comments or suggestions that would be helpful for me in a second edition of this workbook, please feel free to send them my way. While the text and worksheets here are the product of many edits and revisions with input from a range of career experts, frequent interviewers, job seekers and other sources, there is always room for improvements.

Thanks!

# INTRODUCTION

Although we can get caught up in the moment and do not always appreciate the full experience of what we are undertaking, interviewing can be tremendously exciting. Each interview carries within it the possibility of landing in a new role, addressing new challenges, meeting new people and seeing yourself in an entirely different light.

Interviews herald new beginnings. Even if you find interviewing stressful – as I suspect many of you do – you probably also acknowledge that without *some* stress, you may not perform your best. My goal in writing this workbook is to help you mitigate unnecessary stress and drive the interview process, to the extent possible, rather than feel like an unwitting pawn in chess games played by employers large and small.

This workbook grew out of scores of individual and group "interview prep" coaching sessions with clients over the course of 18 months, from C-Suite to junior-level candidates. After reading and recommending to clients various books and articles on interviewing, I realized that none of them captured all of the points I wanted to cover, and some included advice with which I did not even agree.

I began to preface my suggestions with, "Take the advice in this part, but don't read that other part, because it doesn't apply to you." At the same time, I annotated and supplemented my recommendations for successful interviews, which grew into my own 20-page guide. Seeing the results that grew out of this guide and my coaching sessions, I expanded it into individual chapters and provided them to clients, as I continued drafting and revising until completing the workbook you have in your hands today.

This workbook is geared toward strategy. How can you have an organized, thoughtful approach to your interviews? I do not see great value in providing you answers that "work every time," because I don't believe that is an effective strategy. What works in one interview context, with one audience, by one job seeker, may not work in another. What I aim to do instead is give you a framework to understand why some things work and not others, where the "rules" are relatively clear and when and how to adapt when needed.

*Why a workbook?* Because writing something down helps you get your ideas out of your head and onto the page. By doing so, you clarify your thought process, see if there are any gaps in your thinking, unearth complicated emotions, organize yourself and remember your main points in an interview.

## Preview

In private interview preparation sessions with coaching clients, we often spend the first portion of our time together addressing a client's most pressing questions, concerns or stumbling blocks, then move to one or more "mock interviews" and follow up with discussion and feedback. As a preview to the rest of the book, here are some examples of personalized feedback I have given in client sessions, some of which may resonate with you:

*"Your screening interview will be only 20 minutes. How can you tailor your value proposition and hit home the main points in this short time frame?"*

*"Your answers are great, but your responses are too long. Check in with the interviewer [visually or verbally] to make sure you haven't lost him/her."*

*"Your choice of words can make you sound too junior."*

*"Speak to where you are going, not where you have been."*

*"You don't give yourself enough credit for individual contributions. Tell me what you did and where you took the lead, not only what your team accomplished. Your team probably won't be joining you in the new role."*

*"Be authentic but not transparent. You do not need to mention every detail or offer points that are not in your favor. Let's prepare you now so you can be ready to decide, in the midst of an interview, what's appropriate to share."*

*"You are clearly still angry about how it ended at your prior job. What more can we discuss so you are ready to leave your baggage at the door?"*

*"You didn't have any questions ready when I asked what you would like to know about the firm. Let's come up with some ideas so you can find out what you need to know about the role, group, company, etc."*

*"As you are entering into a salary negotiation, you need to know your bottom line before you start the conversation. Do you have certain 'must have' points on the compensation front? How do the pieces – salary, bonus and benefits – fit together?"*

*"If you look away when I ask a question, it may compromise your credibility. How can you be more aware of your body language, especially eye contact?"*

*"If you plan to connect a Skype interview in the room that you are in currently, you should change the lighting so the interviewer can see you better."*

While I clearly cannot give personalized feedback in this workbook – my words are fixed on the page – the exercises are here to help you brainstorm and self-direct. Not every point in the book is applicable to every reader, but I encourage you to use this workbook to <u>dig deep</u> and discover how you can unleash or enhance your <u>inner strategic thinker, planner and doer</u>.

As part of the process, I implore you: don't just read! Write and speak (to someone who is an informed partner and can serve as a sounding board) as you work through these pages. Writing and speaking help us formulate our ideas and clarify for us everything from the complex mental and emotional processes going on inside of us to the entirely straightforward points that we wish to communicate on the given day.

**Part 1** of this workbook covers preparation, from getting the most out of the information and exercises here to cracking the interview code and increasing your interviewing opportunities through networking. Chapter 4 is a high-level view on how to make a game plan for your interviews.

**Part 2** presents four different ways of arriving at your value proposition – namely, through a guided workbook exercise, a core competencies review, a discussion of your particular edge and review of each of these in reference to a specific job. While it is important for you to explore your value proposition at a deeper level, if and when you have the time to do that, an interviewer will often appreciate the direct approach (see Chapter 8). In other words, know your value and be ready to present it, but focus primarily on what problems you can solve for the company or – as they are sometimes referred to colloquially – what employer "pain points" you can address.

**Part 3** covers interview questions, including the capstone question "Why Do You Want to Work Here?" This is a key chapter to read, especially if you are short on time. **Part 4** discusses the unwritten rules of interviewing. These chapters are especially helpful if your have only a short time to prepare, and if so I suggest you scan the topics and highlight those that speak to your immediate needs.

**Part 5** covers final considerations, including interview blocks, confidence boosts and special points in your candidacy that you may want or need to address. I also include some examples of "behind the scenes" factors that may play into an interview and are not always obvious to the job seeker, as well as a final chapter on following up, evaluating offers and negotiating your job package, as well as more technical points such as employee handbooks and noncompetition agreements.

Interviewing seems like a simple thing, at its heart. Many of us agonize for days and weeks, get dressed up on an appointed date, sit in a room for an hour or longer with an interviewer (or group of them) who ask(s) us a series of highly or mildly annoying questions, some of which seem too personal, off-topic, condescending, etc., then play the "waiting game" to see if we made the cut. At least, that's usually the worst version of it. What's not to like, right?

This goal of guide is to help you make your interviews less like the worst-case scenario I describe above and more of an invigorating challenge and opportunity to showcase your talents. After reading and working through this book and completing the associated exercises, I hope you can say (as a good friend of mine told me recently, with her usual touch of witty sarcasm):

*"The truth is, I look forward to interviews because I kill them.*
*I'm aware I'm in a sick minority."*

Even if you already think that you "interview well," you have the chance on these pages to increase your savvy and value proposition, use the interview as an opportunity for due diligence to ensure a fit on your end and make the most informed career move in your next transition.

Here's to your professional future!

# PART 1:

# PREPARATION

# CHAPTER 1
# HOW TO USE THIS WORKBOOK IF...

*Interviews can get very emotional. Sometimes you just need to simplify them into a list of actionable items. Think about what you are trying to achieve and take steps to get there.*
- Financial Services Executive

I am honored to share the interview preparation journey with you.

First and foremost, my goal is to help you target the areas that you wish or need to address regarding the interview process. Of course, this is a printed page rather than a conversation, so I can't quite ask you that directly and write a book based on your responses. What I can do, however, is imagine that you are facing one of a few possible scenarios:

- you have an interview coming up and wanted to brush up on your skills;

- you have not interviewed in over 10 years, and it is a daunting concept;

- while you have met success in some interviews, you have missed the mark on a few coveted roles;

- you are relatively content with your job, but you have been unexpectedly presented with an interview opportunity and have little time to prepare;

- after many failed interviews, the pressure of "putting yourself out there" is becoming unbearable;

- you have never (or almost never) interviewed before in your life; or

- you have interviewed successfully many times, but this next interview is the Big One, and you don't want to blow it.

Regardless of your situation, this workbook can help you meet your goals. This chapter provides a roadmap to prioritize the right sections of this workbook based on your time available and individual needs.

Many of the chapters in this book build on prior chapters. In the best of all possible worlds, you will have an opportunity to read the book in order, consider each section and complete all of the workbook portions. Practically speaking, however, you may either lack the time to read every chapter or not be at a place to make use of certain parts in this book. The best (and worst) part about interviewing is that your next interview could be as soon as tomorrow, so you can keep this workbook on hand for future reference.

## A.   Your Interview Is Tomorrow

Congratulations! If your interview is tomorrow, and you are just picking up this book, here is what I suggest you read first:

*The Table of Contents*

If you scan through the Table of Contents, you can turn to the sections that cover questions you need answered *now*. There is no need to worry at this point about close reading. I have labeled each section so you can quickly find what you need. Your immediate goal is to solve a few "sticking points" that you need to fix by tomorrow. (Don't read too much in one sitting, or you may be overwhelmed.) After that, here is what you can read next:

*Your Interview Strategies and Game Plan* (Chapter 4)

*Your Job-Specific Value Proposition and Tailored Accomplishments* (Chapter 8)

*The Capstone Question: "Why Do You Want to Work Here?"* (Chapter 9)

*"Do You Have Any Further Questions?,"* which appears at the end of *"Your Weaknesses" and Other Tough Questions* (Chapter 10)

After that, if you still have time and can decipher and digest the influx of information and ideas (make sure you get enough sleep!), you can scan through the following chapters, stopping at any section that addresses a point you wish or need to resolve before tomorrow:

*Interviewing 101* (Chapter 11) and *Beyond 101* (Chapter 12)

*Core Competencies That Get You Hired* (Chapter 6)

*"Your Weaknesses" and Other Tough Interview Questions* (the remainder of Chapter 10)

*Breaking Through Interview Blocks* (Chapter 13), if you are filled with dread about your interview

*Addressing Special Considerations in Your Candidacy* (Chapter 14), if any apply

Note: If you will be facing an interview format other than a standard in-person interview, you may also want to read "Be Ready for Skype and Other Formats" in Chapter 12.

Once you have completed tomorrow's interview, you can also read *After the Interview* (Chapter 16) for information about how to follow up, negotiate terms and other steps that follow the interview. Sneak preview: Write a thank-you note. Don't forget.

## B.   Your Interview Is in a Week or Less

If your interview will be held within a week, I would add the following chapters to the list above:

*Behind the Scenes (The Interviewer's Side of the Table)* (Chapter 15)

*Creating Your Value Proposition* (Chapter 5)

*Your Edge* (Chapter 7)

## C.    You Have More Than a Week or Don't Yet Have an Interview

If you have more than a week to prepare for your interviews, I suggest you scan through the book from front to back, identify and read those chapters that are most relevant for your circumstances and complete any workbook portions that help you progress. You also may wish to check the section at the end called "Further Resources" to find additional books that can help you through your own particular sticking points. Finally, if certain chapters raised ideas that you find challenging, you can go back and work through them again.

If you do not yet have an interview and wish to improve your chances of obtaining one, you may wish to focus on *Network Early and Often: Accessing the Hidden Job Market* (Chapter 3). Networking is an undervalued skill, and you can use it to your advantage in the interview process.

## D.    You Have Never (or Seldom) Interviewed

Start with *Interviewing 101* (Chapter 11), *Beyond 101* (Chapter 12), and *The Capstone Question: "Why Do You Want to Work Here?"* (Chapter 9), *"Your Weaknesses" and Other Tough Questions* (Chapter 10) and read on from there as time permits.

*Core Competencies That Get You Hired* (Chapter 6) may also be a particularly helpful chapter if you are new to interviewing, although if you have the time, I would start first with *Creating Your Personal Value Proposition* (Chapter 5) and then read *Your Job-Specific Value Proposition and Tailored Accomplishments* (Chapter 8).

Finally, do not forget to read *After the Interview* (Chapter 16). You do not need to wait until after you have interviewed to read it!

## E.    You Have Had Dozens of Interviews (But Are Rusty)

Start with **Part 3: Interview Questions**, which includes *The Capstone Question: "Why Do You Want to Work Here?"* (Chapter 9) and *"Your Weaknesses" and Other Tough Questions* (Chapter 10). You also may find *Beyond 101: Refining Your Interview Style* (Chapter 12) and *Behind the Scenes (The Interviewer's Side of the Table)* (Chapter 15) particularly helpful.

After that, I suggest that you read **Part 2: Your Value Proposition**, which includes the following chapters: *Creating Your Personal Value Proposition* (Chapter 5), *Core Competencies That Get You Hired* (Chapter 6), *Your Edge* (Chapter 7) *and Your Job-Specific Value Proposition and Tailored Accomplishments* (Chapter 8).

Depending on what else you may need to brush up on, you can continue to read from there. At some point during the course of your interviews, you should also read *After the Interview*

(Chapter 16), especially if you will have the opportunity to evaluate multiple offers and negotiate your compensation and benefits package.

## F.      You Hate to Write in Books

While it is not necessary to do all of the workbook exercises, you will gain more awareness about yourself, as well as internalize and reinforce what you have learned, if you earnestly contemplate and complete the questions. It is tempting to skip the workbook parts to be able to get the book completed more quickly – and I am sure that I have been guilty of that myself on occasion – but remember that insight, not speed, is the goal.

You will better understand the insights here and recall them in the interview if you have not only read the chapters but also expressed the concepts and your personal thoughts in writing.

Go ahead. I have added a few lines here to get your writing-in-the-book feet wet. I have also given you wide margins to make additional notes, if anything strikes you as you are reading.

My burning questions about interviewing that need answers:

_____

_____

_____

_____

My feeling of interview preparedness (on a scale of 1 to 10):

_____

Chapters of this workbook I plan to read first:

_____

_____

Chapters I plan to read in the future:

_____

_____

_____

# CHAPTER 2
# FIRST STEPS TO CRACKING THE INTERVIEW CODE

Above all, this book is about cracking the interview code and becoming a "master interviewee" so that doors open for you at your very next interview and over the course of your career. While that is a tall order, I do my best to meet it.

My goal here is not to show you the "one right way" to interview. It is to communicate an efficient and effective framework so that you can succeed on your own terms.

I know that you may not be seeking (at this juncture) to *master interviewing*, you may only be reading this to *get that next job*, and the interview for that job may be almost upon you. If that's the case and 200+ pages is overwhelming (and overkill) for your purposes at the moment, feel free to revisit the roadmap in Chapter 1 and return here to read once you get your bearings and are able to invest more time.

## A.     Beyond Q&A-Style Interview Prep

Many interview books and other resources on the market are Q&A style (e.g., the top 100 interview questions and formulaic answers). I came across quite a number of them in my background reading for this book. Interview guides that are comprised of hundreds of interviewing questions and sample answers are often great resources to prepare candidates for interviews, although some suggest responses than may not be appropriate for your situation (disclaimers aside).

No Q&A guide, however, addresses the "entire package" of interview preparation and how your answers should be woven into your overall narrative as a candidate. Certainly high-achieving job seekers can prepare with these materials in the same way that they geared up for standardized tests in high school, knowing that if they get enough of the right answers, they can come out ahead of the pack. Yet even high-performers are shortchanged if they do not gain a comprehensive understanding of the interview process and how to successfully <u>and</u> authentically communicate in an interview.

Just as schools that only "teach to the test" are not encouraging students to think for themselves, books that only teach candidates how to adjust their interview answers to the expectations of "the interviewer" (as if there were a standard interviewer, with a uniform set of expectations) do nothing encourage candidates to think for themselves and plan their own careers. Therefore, while interview Q&A guides help calm nerves and encourage good interview etiquette, they do not lay a full foundation for the rigors of the process, because they fail to guide candidates through the professional development needed to truly master interviewing.

At the same time, the wide availability of common interview questions results in an arms' race of sorts, with interviewers and interviewees searching for even tougher questions and more polished responses, respectively, until the entire process becomes an exercise in who has invested more time and energy in being studious about common interview questions rather than an intelligent conversation about whether a candidate is actually right for a role. It also can lead to interviewers asking exceedingly probing questions, not being satisfied with your answers, because they want to get to the raw truth under all that polish.

As one interviewer shared with me:

> *"I never ask the strength/weakness questions myself because they are always rehearsed. People try to give perfect answers (e.g., 'my manager thinks I'm too thorough'). These questions, and the answers I hear in response, just flat out bore me."*

On the other hand, a job seeker shared this advice:

> *"I was on the fourth or fifth round of interviews for a very senior role and finally meeting the CEO. I expected to get some really insightful questions, and I was shocked (and a bit deflated to be honest), when he asked what my weaknesses were. I think I even laughed and said, "Really?" out loud, although I regretted almost immediately having said it. At first, I thought the CEO would smile and move onto another question, but he didn't. I wasn't prepared for the question, and I must have insulted him that I appeared to be judging his interviewing skills (which I clearly was). Needless to say, I did not get the job."*

One of the themes that surfaces many times in this book is to be ready for any type of interview (or interviewer), because often you cannot know until you arrive what you will encounter. That said, the more you know about your interviewer before you arrive, the better off you will be, as long as you don't feel the need to divulge every detail you have learned (and appear a stalker in the process). If you happen to have a common friend or acquaintance who knows your interviewer, by all means call that person and ask for any information that may help your interview. The interviewer will not be suspicious upon hearing you did so but instead take it as a sign of seriousness about the company and role and your ability to obtain and weigh information, considering all the angles, before making significant decisions.

### In My Experience: BE AUTHENTIC

*Early in my career, I interviewed with a team of partners at a financial services firm, including one who would be my direct supervisor (let's call him David) and another who worked closely with him (let's call him Sam).*

*At one point, Sam asked me what type of manager I preferred – hands on or hands off. I had no idea what to answer, and I could sense from his expression this was a critical point for me to get right.*

*I figured that Sam must be asking because he wanted to see if I was a fit for David, but I stalled, saying that I could work with either. (I still determined what type of manager David was, although in retrospect it should have been obvious.)*

*I added that I saw the benefits of both personalities, since one type of manager could act more like a mentor while the other would teach through a sink-or-swim approach. Sam pushed me again to choose which one I preferred, and I deflected again. There were so many positive and negative aspects of each approach, and I didn't want to start rattling off all the things wrong with one or the other, as I didn't want to sound negative. After another minute of hedging my answer, I could see Sam was getting frustrated, but I didn't still want to commit to an answer.*

*Finally, Sam asked what type of manager I didn't like, and I boldly answered, "Honestly, a manager like you might be hard to work with sometimes, because you just don't take 'no' for an answer!" At that point, the pressure was off, and I had a wonderful rest of the interview (and imagined it would be the last time I would see Sam).*

*It was a decisive, authentic and risky response. And sometimes, in the right environment and with the right audience, that works. As was recounted to me years later, that very answer was the reason I got the job. They knew I had the resilience and nerve to succeed in that environment – and was not getting in over my head – traits that served me well in the actual job.*

The most important point I can impart to you in this book is to be authentic in interviews. This does not mean you should be transparent. You do not need to tell your soul's secrets, and certainly you should not. Showing the best version of yourself can lead to great things. Showing someone you are not will only lead to disappointment. While you may "get the job," it will not be worth the stress, falsehoods, need for damage control and other difficulties you will face trying to live up to that initial facade you put forth.

### Be authentic but not transparent.

The best interviewees – whether they learn through trial and error, a studied preparation process or both – are those understand on a fundamental level what interviews are meant to achieve, their limitations and how to come across as an authentic candidate despite the inherent awkwardness of the interview format.

## B.    Be Ready for an Interview Any Day

If you read the above, you may be thinking:

*"I could get smarter about the fundamental purpose of an interview, but I will leave that to someone else. I don't care about the how's and why's of interviewing. I just want the job."*

The problem is that the interview for the "ideal job" (however *you* define it) may come calling when you least expect it.

Five days, weeks or years from now you may get the call of your life and be asked on a Friday to come in for an interview the following Monday with the CEO (or Board of Directors) of a company you have been dying to work for. Oh, and did I mention that your cousin's wedding or other significant event is the same weekend that you need to prepare? This is not just a hypothetical. It could easily happen, especially as you expand your ability to network and talent for being in the right place at the right time.

We all need to crack the interview code – not only take half-baked measures here and there to prepare – so that we can be *ready to interview for a life-changing opportunity any day of our lives*. This applies to everyone at any stage of career, from a stay-at-home mom re-entering the workforce or entry-level college graduate with little employment history to the CEO of a multi-billion dollar company or high-level governmental official and everyone in between. Whatever level of success you have achieved, you will benefit from thinking about how that success can be leveraged into a new opportunity.

Prepping questions and answers is important, but it only gets us so far and usually serves as a short-term solution. If we can see the "questions behind the questions," however, we can get to the heart of the process. At the same time, we can learn to read the clues that interviewers give about the environment at a target employer, avoiding critical missteps when a so-called *dream job* turns into a *nightmare* that we should have seen coming.

While a common goal in completing this workbook is to become a "master interviewee," this it is never the ultimate goal. The chief purpose of mastering interviews is to have mobility and flexibility, so you are never stuck for long in a job that you no longer want. If you can interview well, you are golden. You can create the ability to continue to grow, get out of bad situations, pursue new interests, relocate geographically (or stay within your own community, if you prefer) and rise to the challenge as new opportunities present themselves.

In other words, the learning here is not only "interview prep" for the sake of getting your next job, it is how to master the language of interviewing so that doors will be opened to you over the course of your career.

## C.    What Your Interviewer Really Wants to Know

I mentioned above that an interview for your dream job could drop out of thin air at any moment, leaving you unprepared. Even if this never happens, there is a second, more significant problem with only piecemeal preparation (e.g., reviewing common interview questions) rather than taking a step back to think about interviewing fundamentals. A smart interviewer is not chiefly concerned that you "walk him/her through your resume" or the exact answer to "what are your weaknesses?" or other questions that are commonly asked in the interview process. For many jobs, your interviewer really wants to know the following (or some version of it):

- *Can you do the job?*

- *Are you a good fit?*

- *Will you make my life easier?*

- *Will you solve the problems I really need solved?*

- *Will you make or save the company "real money"?*

- *Can you extrapolate and analogize, or will you waste time and resources (mine and others) because you don't know how to think for yourself?*

- *Will you anticipate issues before they arise and figure out how to fix them?*

- *Will you know how to communicate in a way that people understand (especially me) and on a timely basis?*

- *Can I put you in front of my SVP, EVP, CEO, Board of Directors and/or clients, if and when the time comes?*

- *Can you grow over time if/when our needs progress?*

- *Will you have the resilience to charge through the inevitable setbacks that arise in any job and specifically in the environment in which we operate?*

- *Are you able to manage stress (your own and others) in a positive way?*

- *Will you make me regret hiring you one day?*

- *Will you quit in three months?*

- *Will you bail when there's a crucial deadline?*

- *Will you understand and care about what we are trying to achieve?*

- *Will you get things done?*

- *Can I afford you?*

- *Why should I (take a risk and) hire you?*

Of course, most of the questions above are not standard interview fare in most (if not all) roles. Imagine an interviewer saying:

*"I have just one question:*

*Will you make my life easier and by how much?*
*$150,000 a year easier? Sold! When can you start?"*

Skilled interviewers have a dilemma, in other words. They know that if they asked the above questions directly, the answer to most of them would be an emphatic yes or no, as applicable. Easy peasy, as the phrase goes. Any job seeker could give the right answers to sail through an interview like that, so there is no point in asking. So interviewers ask other questions – such as "what is your ideal job?" – that approximate what they want to discover about the candidate, knowing that many of these questions are poor proxies for what they really want to know yet hoping that the questions they *do* ask get them there.

As a job candidate, the above questions (i.e., the ones a skilled interview would ask, if he/she could) are good ones to keep front of mind. Why? Because these underlying concerns, along with the traits I mention in Chapter 10 that tough interview questions are designed to uncover, will help you recognize what you must demonstrate and address to be hired.

When interviewers ask *"how you overcame a setback in your professional career,"* for example, they are asking for about problem-solving skills and resilience. Any details that you give about the situation should demonstrate those two factors. At the same time, you should be careful that your answer does not demonstrate a propensity to blame others or reveal company or individual confidences, both of which are potential red flags that will peak the ears of an interviewer and damage your candidacy.

The last question from the above list is really the deciding one in any job interview: why should I hire you? I tell my interview preparation clients that every answer they give in an interview should answer this underlying question:

*Why should I hire you?*

If you know and can internalize that "why should I hire you?" is the underlying question behind all other interview questions, you have a huge advantage in the interview process. You won't be tempted to go off on a tangent or give the "wrong" response, because you will always gear your answer to why the interviewer should hire you.

Then again, a large part of why job candidates cannot answer that question is because they have never sat down and asked it of themselves: Why should an employer hire me? What value do I add? Job seekers are often focused on getting out of where they are and see the next role as an exit strategy more than an opportunity.

*The next role is an opportunity. Not just an exit strategy.*

In Chapters 5 through 8, we work through that underlying question of why an employer should hire you, based on groundwork from now through the end of Chapter 4. The answer is called your "value proposition" and it represents what you can offer to a company as a return on their investment in you as an employee. If you just cannot wait to get started working on your value proposition, feel free to turn to those chapters now.

## D.     The Unskilled or Devious Interviewer

We discussed above the dilemma facing smart interviewers. They have very specific hiring criteria. Above all, they want to know if you'll do the job right, be creative and pragmatic, solve problems effectively, communicate well and get things done.

Not all interviewers are smart, however, as you may have already realized over the years. Some of them are not very smart in general, truth be told, and others are simply not prepared to conduct an effective interview.

As a client wrote to me recently about an interview experience that he had:

> *"The first two interviewers had clearly never looked at my resume before our interview. They were flipping through it and making up questions on the spot, except the questions were very much Interviewing 101, as if they had googled 'how to interview job candidates' and were applying those suggestions, like sticky notes, to various items on my resume: 'So tell me about your biggest challenge at … Job A!' It felt very much like a waste of my time."*

As a job candidate, you not only need to jump through the hoops of a smart interviewer, you also must be prepared to answer the questions of an unskilled interviewer. One way to do this is to keep a subtle eye on the clock and make sure that, toward the end of the conversation (e.g., 45 minutes into an expected one-hour interview), you offer, "Would you like me to explain what I bring to this position?" If the interview is truly horrible, you may need to take charge earlier, so that a meaningful exchange actually takes place, but be careful not to appear that you have a need to control. It's a subtle dance, like most aspects of the interview process.

Finally, some interviewers don't really care about the fate of the company or their group, are about to quit their job themselves, hate their boss, are a horrible judge of character, see you as competition or otherwise are not in the best position to act as an interviewer. In other words, you can have a hostile, devious or careless interviewer just as easily as a smart or unskilled one, and you never know who or what you are going to get until you walk through the door.

## E.     The Job Seeker's Dilemma

The job seeker's dilemma is not unlike the interviewer's dilemma. A shrewd job candidate also has a list of questions he/she wants to ask in an interview but cannot always ask directly, without appearing unprofessional. These questions are the flip side to those a skilled interviewer would like to ask of a future supervisor, such as:

- *Can I do the job?*

- *Is it a good fit?*

- *Will you make my life difficult?*

- *Will I have the opportunity to solve the problems that really need solving?*

- *Will I be given an opportunity to make or save the company "real money"?*

- *Can you lead and manage a team, or will you waste time and resources (mine and others) because you don't know how to supervise properly?*

- *Will you anticipate issues before they arise or blame me afterwards if/when things don't work out?*

- *Will you know how to communicate in a way that people understand (especially me) and on a timely basis?*

- *Do your clients (internal and external) like you?*

- *Will you put me in front of your SVP, EVP, CEO, Board of Directors and/or clients, if and when the time comes?*

- *Will you help me grow over time as my skill level progresses?*

- *Will my resilience to charge through the inevitable setbacks that arise in any job, and specifically in the environment in which we operate, be rewarded?*

- *Are you able to manage stress (your own and others) in a positive way?*

- *Will you make me regret taking this job one day?*

- *Will you fire me in three months?*

- *Will you crush me to pieces when there's a crucial deadline?*

- *Will you understand and care about what I am trying to achieve?*

- *Will you make yourself accessible so I can get things done?*

- *Will you reward me for what I'm worth?*

- *Why should I (take a risk and) work for you?*

Like the interviewer, the job seeker cannot be entirely upfront in an interview process and therefore must ask questions that approximate what he/she wants to know. Also like the interviewer, the job seeker is well served knowing these questions beforehand – see the end of Chapter 10 for a further discussion on the role of job-seeker interview questions – so that the interview can yield a good match.

## F.    Note to New Graduates

If you have read the above job-seeker "true questions" – which are not the same questions you would ask in an interview – and feel that some of them go beyond your current circumstances, I suggest you keep a copy of the list to pull out at a later date. As your career progresses over time, you will find that the questions further resonate with you. You should know from the outset that much of your success in a job is based on your ability to "manage up," and many of these questions try to judge how easy or difficult that will be.

While it is important to know that a job is a JOB and we cannot always fashion it into what we want it to be – our obvious alternative is to find a different job – we also can get better at finding the right fit if we know what we expect from a job and whether those expectations are realistic given the totality of the role we are seeking.

## G.    The Goal of Interview Preparation

We have now painted with the broad brush the goal of interview preparation: to be ready to roll with the punches in an interview setting and demonstrate you are the one for the job, while gaining insight into whether the role is a fit on your end.

While it helps to have rehearsed answers to common questions (and I have given you a guide in Chapters 9 and 10 and there are many other resources available on how to do that), you are clearly aware that the interview is not a controlled environment in which interviewers stick to the list you have prepared. They may just ask you what emergency procedures you would follow if you suddenly needed to land an airplane (even if you are interviewing for a job completely unrelated to aviation) or another seemingly "off the wall" question. Sometimes, these questions are posed because the interviewer has no idea how to get to the issues that matter. Other times, the interviewer has a targeted agenda to see how your mind works (e.g., in a risk-reward environment that requires quick decision-making, how do you fare?). Rather than get flustered or frustrated, your goal is always to answer that same fundamental question:

*Why should I hire you?*

# CHAPTER 3
# NETWORK EARLY AND OFTEN: ACCESSING THE HIDDEN JOB MARKET

*Most job seekers think you get a job by hiding in the dark, submitting resumes for openings posted on the Internet, and hoping for the best. Wrong, wrong, wrong. You get jobs by talking to people. This has to be your strategy.*

- Donald Asher, *Cracking the Hidden Job Market*

*Most people have seen examples of networking, or people talking about networking, that seemed offensive or cheesy. If that's the image you hold, you can decide you're above it. You might imagine you're a better person for not engaging in such things. However, if you withdraw and fail to network, you will damage your career.*

- Michael F. Melcher, *The Creative Lawyer*

As you are preparing your interview strategy, consider this: the majority of jobs are filled through the "hidden job market." As we are discussing the interview process more generally throughout the book, this chapter focuses on how to grow your network and get more interviews. At the same time, targeted networking can bring you more potential points of contact with your interviewers through an expanded set of mutual connections.

## A.    The Hidden Job Market

*What is the hidden job market?* The words "hidden job market" signify that portion of roles that are filled without the use of traditional means such as job postings. In other words, people get connected personally to interviewers without the need to submit (other than, in some cases, as a formality) their candidacy to the "black hole" of online resume submissions. Hidden does not mean inaccessible; on the contrary, jobs that are obtained through knowing someone are highly accessible, if you are know how to find and use the right channels. This chapter is about learning how to do that.

While many candidates spend vast amounts of their time searching job boards – populating fields, sending in resumes and hoping for the best – the better networked ones are getting more interviews and landing more jobs through personal connections. They may also apply through the traditional channels, but the majority of their job search efforts are devoted to putting themselves in front of decision-makers to apply for jobs that have not been advertised or, in some cases, even created yet. By getting and keeping in touch with their extended network, recruiters and companies directly, they are front of mind when a need or request arises. The question asked by a CEO or department head, "do you know anyone who…?" is answered, "yes, I know Donna and [insert your name here]. Would you like me to contact them and ask if either may be interested in talking to us?"

The same proficiencies that will make you successful in accessing the hidden job market will help you succeed in interviews. The first step is to realize that **people hire people**. Computer algorithms may sort scores of resumes, but they are notoriously poor at identifying candidates whose experience does not "read" (algorithmically) as a very close match to the job posting. Algorithms cannot get a gut feeling for a candidate or read between lines on a resume. In other words, applicant tracking systems screen out a lot of potentially good candidates and may suggest a number of others who are not, in the final analysis, a true match.

Hands down, people are more likely to hire someone who comes recommended than take a candidate who has no connection to them, and in fact the jobs that are filled through traditional means are often the ones for which no suitable candidates turned up from a word-of-mouth search. (Even in those cases in which a job posting must be made public and open to all, such as government positions, the job seekers who know someone on the inside can get their file flagged and put on the right desk at the top of the pile.) As a candidate, if you can leverage your network to make connections at your target employers, you will have more interviews, and they will more likely turn into job offers.

## B.    Networking

> *Stop committing random acts of networking.*
> - J. Kelly Hoey, Networking Expert

Networking is a way of more formally organizing the people you know, and the people they know, to create a web of contacts for the exchange of information, advice, contacts and support. If you invest in the process, your network will support you for your entire career.

You can meet people anywhere who can be helpful to your career, from a job fair to a Starbucks. You only need to be open to the possibilities and ready to present yourself as a serious and viable candidate when the opportunity arises. That takes confidence, yes. Find it.

I must admit that, in the early years of my career, I completely undervalued networking in my job search and during the interview process. I faced exactly the same problems and fears as many of my clients:

- I agonized over how or whether to connect with people I did not know well, worried that I was bothering them with my requests.

- When I did connect, I sometimes blundered the communications, not getting to the point about who I was, how I could help them or they could help me and why they should invest their time in me.

- I did not understand the "give to get" concept of networking.

- I did not appreciate the value of long-term relationships and saw networking as much more of a short-lived, almost transactional exercise.

- I hated selling myself.

- So I scrolled through endless job posts, thinking that if I applied to enough of them, playing the odds that someone would recognize what a great candidate I was, and the interviews would start rolling in.

Networking is often an Achilles' heel for job candidates. As sales coach Carolyn Herfurth, CEO and Founder of The Biztruth, always says, "*You may be able to sell a million other things, but it doesn't mean you have learned how to sell yourself.*" Often people think that networking is an elusive skill that only serves those who are "true networkers" (whatever that means), went to the best schools, join the right (expensive) clubs or know how to play a secret game.

It is absolutely true that you need to "fish where the fish are" in terms of prioritizing your networking efforts to places that you are likely to meet people who can help you. At the same time, not everyone needs to network with top business leaders at every turn in order to make their efforts effective. Your networking contacts do not need power. What they need is access, influence and the motivation to help you. Alex from the accounting department at Company A (whose son is in the same Boy Scout troop as yours) may be able to introduce you to Cynthia who heads up the marketing team. Trish who runs the mailroom at Company B (and happens to be your neighbor) may have a great rapport with the CEO and put in a good word for you that gets your resume read or could tip the balance in your interview. Sundeep who has his own company (and you met at the gym) may have a network of clients and contacts that could be helpful. The only way you can find out is to get to know people, build trust and grow authentic relationships based on mutual respect.

*Network early and often. Your career is not a sprint but a marathon.*

Keep an open channel with your connections and do not limit your networking to your close friends (who may have the same information you do and a similar network to yours). Seek people out who hold value for you, and find a way to provide value in return. This is the idea behind "give-to-get" networking.

Offering something of value to your contacts is what really builds momentum rather than, as I mentioned above, "transactional" networking based on a one-time need. If your only interest in a person is so that he/she can get you a job, and after that you do not care if you see or contact that person again, that is using someone as a means to an end. While networking may have evolved over the years, care and etiquette have not. Unfortunately, many job seekers are so afraid of the *appearance* of using someone that they fail to network altogether, missing important opportunities. The cure for this concern is to follow up, maintain relationships and offer value to your network rather than only leveraging your network for your own ends.

So what *can* you offer of value in return, whether you are a database administrator, bank teller, student, chief financial officer, executive vice president or otherwise? Actually, the value can arise in a professional context or be completely unrelated to the workplace. First and foremost, you can show that you *actually value* the person, which sounds simple enough. Make time for conversation. Know who they are and what is important to them.

As one executive said to me recently about a networking experience:

> *"I went out to lunch with someone recently who asked me if I was taking the family skiing in Vermont this year. I answered 'no, we don't ski very much,' and he artfully switched gears to another topic. I later realized that our last ski trip was a few years ago, just weeks before the last time I met for lunch with this same individual. I had probably gushed about how much fun we had on the trip and it went right into his (relationship management) notes, which he pulled up to read before meeting with me again. Although I realized what he was doing, I didn't feel 'played' but appreciated his interest and was actually impressed that he moved on to another topic without skipping a beat. He's clearly a good networker but genuine at the same time."*

Second, find a way that you can support your network. Everyone needs something, whether it is encouragement, kindness or a more tangible need. Maybe the person you have met is just getting into gardening, and you can offer your tips or bring him/her a new small plant or herb. With others, your return value could be helping a friend or relative with a problem (big or small) that you are uniquely positioned to solve or simply being supportive of an idea, cause or change in that person's life. If you are paying attention, you will not need anyone to generate ideas for you on how to connect more deeply with your network. The ways will become obvious as you open up, show concern, listen and engage.

If you start to network more intentionally, sometimes you may get it wrong, but often you will get it right. The more you do it, the less it will feel forced, especially if you focus your attention on the individual rather than yourself. If you can build a relationship of trust with people you actually care about, and have this network available at the time your next round of interviews comes, the "ask" for how they can help you becomes much easier. In addition, they will want to help you, because they know that one day when they are in need, you will be there.

It is important that you gear your networking efforts to people you like and trust. It is nearly impossible to build a rapport with someone if you are suspicious of his/her motives. If you would be uncomfortable or unwilling to help on your end, the two-way street becomes a traffic jam, leading to hard feelings and broken promises.

Seek out a network of good people. There are more than enough to choose from.

Contacts that would be most helpful to me:

_____

_____

What I can offer my network:

_____

_____

Ways I can expand my network:

_____

_____

I would network more if:

_____

_____

I can make that happen by:

_____

_____

## C.      Leadership and Volunteering

Taking leadership roles and volunteering are great ways to expand your network and open up more opportunities to connect with potential employers, whether you are involved in activities within your field or across fields. Working with others on a worthwhile, common goal leads to a more significant bond than a hundred lunch dates.

For job seekers, know that these roles take a strong commitment and are about the cause, not about you. You are indeed building your network, experience and skills over the long term, but you should not expect that leadership or volunteer roles "pay off" with immediate job prospects.

### Coaching Moment

*I will never forget a potential client, a woman in her 50s (let's call her Mary), who came into my office and announced that she was doing all the right things and did not know why they were not leading to a job. I asked Mary what she was doing, and she mentioned volunteering as an example. Someone had been suggested it would be useful in her job search, and Mary dutifully complied. "I have been there once a week for six months, and it is so frustrating. I keep saying to everyone that I am unemployed, but they haven't found me anything. I think I am going to quit, because it is just a waste of my time." I gently asked Mary if the work she was doing as a volunteer, which sounded like it really made a difference in people's lives, was meaningful to her. "No, not really," she admitted. I then asked if she felt she had made any strong connections with the other volunteers over the past six months. "No, they kind of seem distant," she answered.*

*I realized rather quickly into our conversation that Mary was wearing her pain on her sleeve, alienating her family, friends and colleagues by making each moment about what others could do for her (and were not, in her estimation, doing quickly or effectively enough) rather than creating any reciprocity in her relationships. While she was doing the "right things" as she said, she was doing them with the wrong spirit and overtly broadcasting to the world that her good deeds were merely a means to an end.*

*Unfortunately for Mary, her goals did not become closer through her efforts but further away as a result.*

## D.   LinkedIn®

Another great source of networking, as well as job leads, is LinkedIn. At the time of this writing, LinkedIn is an incredibly powerful tool and a key source for online networking in many professional fields, with a self-reported 100 million active users and a high ranking in Google search results. Although there are some complaints that its usefulness is diminished with the increased prevalence of sponsored posts and subjects that are better suited to Facebook, for the foreseeable future, LinkedIn is here to stay.

You should review your LinkedIn profile to make sure it supports the "branding statement" that you make in your interviews. While your resume can (and should) be tweaked for each application, you only get one shot at LinkedIn.

If your branding message differs from one interview to the next, you will need your LinkedIn profile and other online materials to bridge across these individual iterations and support every version of the value proposition that you present. While the data varies on how often recruiters and hiring managers check LinkedIn profiles of candidates they are interviewing, depending on the industry and who is doing the reporting, you should assume that it is more likely than not your profile will be reviewed. In that same vein, take a spin of your general online reputation as well, to see how the "rest of you" checks out.

In the context of using LinkedIn for job leads and interviews, you should know and decide from among two basic approaches. First, if you have an inviting and well-defined profile, you may *generate* interest from recruiters, who can come to your page and seek you out for a suitable role. Second, even if your profile is not complete, it should be professional so that when recruiters and hiring managers who *have already received* your resume or application visit your page, they can *confirm* you are the right candidate rather than have cause for concern. You can think of these two approaches "lead generation" and "lead verification," respectively, as these terms are used in the context of search engine optimization (SEO) for webpages. Lead generation means to generate interest directly through the content on the page, while lead verification means to serve as a confirmation tool after leads are generated through another means, such as offline networking.

There is no true definition of a "100% complete" LinkedIn profile, because it differs among candidates based on their individual experiences. Some may have publications or patents, for example, where others will not. There are, however, certain ways that you can create a rich profile that will attract attention that can lead to interviews. These include:

- *Have an inviting image so that people click on your profile* – Include a recent photo in which you are friendly and smiling, the lighting is good, you do not look "stiff" and your attire is professional. Also, I beg you not to include someone else who is cropped out of one side of the image. (This point needs attention from one too many LinkedIn users who think a recent photo with their spouse or partner would be a good choice to adapt to a professional setting). In addition to more user views, LinkedIn boosts the profiles of its members who include a photo (even a poor one).

Above all, ask yourself two questions about your profile photograph:

(1) *Does this image match my current personal brand?*

(2) *If I were head of one of my target organizations, would I send myself (as I appear in this photo) to meet with its best clients?*

- *Create a compelling and appropriate headline* – You want to include engaging keywords (not only job titles) in your headline so that you are found and visited by your target audience.

- *Write a strong, keyword-rich summary* – Your summary should not be a simple recitation of your resume. Create a narrative that draws in the reader while expressing your personal value proposition (i.e., what you offer as a candidate, discussed further in Part 2 of this workbook). Even if you are in the press extensively or otherwise have a robust online presence, your LinkedIn summary is a key place (in addition to your website, which you can reference in the summary) where you can control your professional brand.

- *Include experience sections that are accessible and highlight keywords* – Your experience sections should also invite the reader by being highly focused and readable, emphasizing your accomplishments in each role. At the same time, include keywords in your experience section as well. If a recruiter is searching for a biochemist in Seattle, he/she will likely use the words "biochemist" and "Seattle" in the search. It may sound obvious, but there are many sparse profiles that miss the obvious steps. Finally, if you have a specialty beyond biochemistry, for example, such as genetics, nutrition or clean energy, those keywords should also be in your profile.

- *Add connections* – I do not recommend openly connecting with everyone who sends a request. Your network should reflect meaningful associations rather than just that you have a "Connect" button and know how to use it. In this sense, I part ways with so-called LinkedIn open networkers (LIONs). While you want a robust network so that you rise in search results – as LinkedIn highlights $1^{st}$, $2^{nd}$ or $3^{rd}$ degree connection or mutual group member in a search – you also want to be able to explain how you know someone, and speak confidently about who is in your network, if asked by an interviewer about your mutual connections (i.e., those people to whom you are both connected on LinkedIn). In addition, there are valid concerns about trolls and fake accounts, so take caution with whom you connect.

When you seek to add others as connections, take care to write a personalized request. For the reasons above and due to the number of requests many LinkedIn users receive, if you do not have a note about why you wish to connect – unless it would be obvious given the context – your request may be ignored or deleted.

- *Seek recommendations* – Meaningful recommendations from professional connections, especially senior talent who know you well, are helpful to create credibility.

Much more can be said about how to manage your LinkedIn account and leverage it to increase your likelihood for interviews, and please feel free to contact me directly (details in the front pages of this book) if you would like further materials on or information about LinkedIn.

Top ways I can improve my profile:

_____

_____

Note: If you are a novice on LinkedIn, its proprietary index of assistance on common topics is very robust. In addition, there are many third-party websites that help you with topics, including some that I have covered on my own blog. A simple Google or other search engine entry for "LinkedIn" and the topic you need to research should get you to the information you need. For example, if I run a Google search on "LinkedIn turn off notifications," the first result I see is an article on PopSugar entitled, "How to Stop Notifying Everyone When Updating Your LinkedIn," by Emily Co, which is available at <http://www.popsugar.com/smart-living/How-Stop-Notifications-When-Updating-LinkedIn-Profile-30420705>.

## E.    Help Your Connections Help You

The best way to help your connections help you is to know and communicate what you wish to achieve. "I am looking for a job, can you help?" does not provide specific enough information to be helpful. While it may tug at heartstrings, as we all want our friends to do well, only your very closest friends will set devote time and energy to go that extra mile and try to figure out *how* exactly to help you. In addition, as I said above, they may not be in the best situation to do that, having a lot of the same connections and information that you do.

Try instead, in the context of a larger message that goes beyond *your* needs, saying:

> *"I have four years of experience with X, and I am looking for a job doing Y or Z. Do you know anyone who may have advice or information for me?"*

Feel free to get into more specifics, but don't drag it out into four or five paragraphs about your situation. Be polite, make the X, Y and Z sufficiently descriptive and get to the point about what you offer (as a candidate) and what you need (in terms of a good fit). In other words, if you want results, don't waste anyone's time. Do the hard work. Make it easy for your contacts to help you.

If you have not yet determined what you offer and what you need, I suggest that you take steps to clarify that first (see Chapters 5 to 8), so you can present yourself as a stronger candidate when you do reach out to your connections.

My current message to contacts:

_____

_____

How I can improve that message:

_____

_____

_____

_____

## F.   Informational Interviews

If you have heard the term "informational interviews," you nonetheless may have been puzzled about what these actually are and how they work. Informational interviews are not "pre-interviews." At times they can lead to an actual job interview with the same or another company, but the premise of an informational interview is that you are there to seek information (hence the name), not shake trees looking for a job to fall out or pump the contact to plug you for an open opportunity. An informational interview can help you:

- Learn about the specifics of a certain role or industry
- Decide among different occupations or choose a specialty
- Give you a chance to move out of your comfort zone
- Focus your career goals
- Discover new roles that you did not know existed
- Ask questions that can help you prepare for your career
- Possibly arrange an opportunity to visit an employer and see people "in action"
- Polish your interviewing skills

You can set up informational interviews by asking for introductions or contacting people directly. While not everyone will be receptive, many people enjoy sharing their knowledge and encouraging others to progress in their field. Find a way to connect with the person, whether it is through common interests or a genuine desire to work in their field or setting.

Informational interviews generally run 20-30 minutes and are best conducted in person, although phone interviews work as well, especially for busy professionals. At times, you can request a phone interview first and then, after the person gets to know you, follow up with a thank-you note and request for an in-person meeting if and when the individual's schedule permits (which may be shortly after the first conversation or months later, so remember to stay in touch). If your request for an informational interview is granted, follow the same formalities as a job interview, and be ready for the possibility that you may be introduced to others at the same office, so leave more time available than you have scheduled for the meeting.

Whether it is an informational interview request or other point of contact, don't be shy about reaching out. The old adage is true (as long as you don't become a pest): the worst anyone can say is no. Ask your contacts who else might be able to help you understand more about a particular field, industry or role, and if they mention something interesting, you can research it and reach out directly, whether or not they have additional contacts there.

Also, if you do have a suggested connection that turns into a great meeting, don't forget to thank the person who referred you. This keeps the cycle going! At times you just need a reason, any legitimate reason, to reach out and keep the connection alive, so a heartfelt thank you (and assumedly you <u>will</u> really mean it) is a great way to do that.

The following types of informational interviews would be helpful to me:

_____

_____

I can arrange them through:

_____

_____

Questions I can ask in informational interviews include:

_____

_____

_____

Early readers of this book have asked for help answering the last workbook exercise above. *What questions should you ask in informational interviews?* The appropriate questions vary depending on why you are having the interview, with whom you are meeting, and so on. Start by asking yourself what you hope to get out of the meeting. Are you trying to decide between different industries or fields? Persuade someone to recommend you for a role? Flesh out more information about a particular company? While it is never effective to wear your heart on your sleeve (e.g., "I have no idea what to do with my life. Can you help me?"), you are there to gather information, so ask targeted questions to do that, even if it does mean admitting that you need help sorting things out (regardless of how senior you may be).

For example, I have worked with high-level individuals transitioning out of government, military or other institutional roles into the corporate world, and their questions center often around how to make that transition efficiently and effectively. They use informational interviews among other means to identify and cure their own blind spots about how this new environment "speaks" and operates, what it values (generally it intends to make a profit, but what else?), who its key players are, where they can make further contacts and the like. To do so, they must admit what they don't know and be ready for new learning, realizing that their aptitude is high and clear, they only need guidance to put the right pieces into place and fully leverage opportunities. That is the right approach generally to informational interviews. Be equal parts confident of your abilities and open to new suggestions.

Here are some more ideas for informational interview questions, to be tailored to your circumstances and the person with whom you are meeting. (Please do not simply recite the questions below but take some time to think about whether they are appropriate or if there are better questions to ask in a specific case. Also, if you do not understand the purpose of asking one or more of the questions below, find out or don't ask it!)

Note: If you direct your questions to someone's current or a former company, spend some time preparing (e.g., 30 minutes) and make sure that you do not ask any questions that can be answered through a simple online search and review of the company's website. The last thing that you want to do is waste a contact's time reciting information that you could have figured out yourself. Neither will you get much out of the meeting nor will you make a good impression.

Examples of general questions about the company:

*I have been reading that [Name of Company] has re-envisioned itself not as [X] but rather as [Y]. Can you tell me more about that?*

*I see that [Name of Company] has grown from 10 to 50 employees in the last year. Wow! Can you tell me what's behind the growth, other than what I can read in the news?*

*Would you say that [Name of Company] is more of a collaborative work environment or one that values individual contributions?*

*How does [Name of Company] decide where to focus its efforts next?*

*What is it like day-to-day in your [department, group, etc.]?*

*[If the person is involved with interviewing] What is a typical interview with [Name of Company] like?*

Examples of general questions about the person:

*I am making a list of publications to read so that I can get a better handle on this new industry. What do you read stay current in the market? Are there particular conferences I should attend?*

*How did you find your role at [Name of Company]? What do you like most about working there?*

*Do you have a mentor at [Name of Company]? Have mentors (or sponsors) been an important part of your career? How did you find and build those relationships?*

Note in the last question above that sponsors are different from mentors. Mentors help with professional growth and in making connections, while sponsors promote an individual for advancement (by vouching for the person and/or "spending" accumulated political capital within the firm to push a candidate over others for the same role).

Examples of specific questions you may have:

*I am trying to figure out the best way to present the fact that I want to be in a smaller, more entrepreneurial environment, even though my recent roles have been at larger companies. What should I be thinking about?*

*Do you know if they only hire candidates with engineering or science degrees for this role, or is it enough to have sales experience with similar products?*

*How do you suggest I sort out [or prioritize] the different types of opportunities available to me at this point in my career? [Be ready to give some examples of X or Y. Do not ask about too wide a range or something outside of the person's expertise. Save that for another informational interview with the appropriate person.]*

*If you were me, based on what you know [from my resume], what next steps would you take?*

## G.     Don't Expect Too Much, Too Soon

As I mentioned above, when going out to your network, I suggest you ask for advice or information about your job search rather than expecting someone to immediately connect you with an opportunity. As I often say to my clients, your network cannot manufacture a job where none exists. If someone feels you would be a good candidate, knows you are looking and is comfortable putting you up for the role, simply mentioning that you are in the market should be enough to get the process started.

Remember that your contacts are only going to recommend you for a job if: (1) they think you are good candidate, (2) they know you are looking for that specific job and recall it when the opportunity presents itself to recommend someone, and (3) they are comfortable putting you up for the opportunity.

On the last point, everyone has a different comfort level at which he/she feels comfortable making recommendations to their employer. I have spoken with clients, for example, who are beyond distraught that a close friend will not recommend them for a job in the friend's company. The truth is that often you will not get a straight answer from someone about the source of his/her hesitation. It could be a credibility issue on your end – i.e., a worry by your friend that anyone he/she recommends could come back to reflect poorly on him/her – or something entirely unrelated, such as an issue within the company that makes it a negative work environment (which your friend nonetheless is not comfortable sharing with you) or a simple desire to keep work and home life separate. Relationships can be complicated, so take a step back and look at the larger picture. If one of your contacts is unwilling to make a recommendation, forcing the issue will unlikely bring the intended result and may even alienate the individual, who could then recommend *against* hiring you. Find another way into the company or seek out another opportunity altogether.

## H.    Recruiters

An important part of the mix to increase your chance of getting interviews – and succeed once you have them – is to work with recruiters in your field who have access to jobs that may be a good match for you. I suggest that you work on building relationships with trusted recruiters early in your career, if possible, so they will remember you when they have a lead. Pick up their calls, be respectful and make recommendations of friends or colleagues (if appropriate and the individuals are amenable to you sharing their name and information). Out of the three main employers I have had in my career, for example, one of them came directly out of my name being shared by a colleague with a recruiter with whom I stayed in touch every few months, even though I was not looking for a new opportunity at the time of our initial call.

Recruiters, as career professionals, are poised to give you feedback on the market, compensation ranges and other points. If you work with them on a placement, they can also help you negotiate terms with an employer, as I will discuss further in the last chapter (After the Interview).

Remember that most recruiters are paid by employers to find candidates, so their goals are to find a suitable candidates for open roles. This means many things in practice, not least of which is that most recruiters are not in the business of creating roles for available candidates (and therefore may need to be politely pursued if you are on the job hunt). It also means that they are not your mother or your therapist. If you want to be considered a "fee worthy" candidate – one that can be placed and will earn them their fee – then you have to show up as someone who will present well in the interview and have a good chance of being hired. Recruiters cannot present candidates to employers who make them look bad or waste the employers' time, or they will quickly be out of clients.

## I.    Direct Contact with Employers

In your attempt to increase your interview-per-application ratio, you can also connect directly with the people who are in a position to hire you. While this may not always be as productive at a Fortune 100 company or major financial institution – although it can be, if you find the right "hook" and a receptive audience – there are a multitude of smaller employers who are delighted to have candidates show a proactive interest in working for them. Talk to someone who is knowledgeable about the industry – and, if possible, the company or person – to determine the best approach to take and message to convey. Also, *always try to send your application directly to a person.* If not, it is unlikely to be read.

Sending documents by regular mail also works with some companies, especially for a mid-level or junior candidate who needs that extra edge and does not have the luxury of time to develop a rich network as described in this chapter. If 100 candidates submit resumes by email and two submit a second copy by regular mail, for example, those two candidates may have increased their odds of getting their applications in front of the right person.

While the recipient may simply put the mailed resume in the same pile as other resumes (or, in limited circumstances, the trash), he/she may also take the opportunity to read it more closely, especially if the cover letter is compelling and/or the resume is adept at emphasizing what this particular interviewer is seeking in a job candidate. Finally, if there is no opening at the time and the resume goes into a "hold" file, you can imagine that it will stand out (on professional paper) against all of the emailed-and-printed versions.

Note here the caveat that some job openings request "email only," so you should respect the rules of the game (and not use direct mail or call to follow up). Also, only use the print-and-mail option if you are comfortable with your information being opened first by an administrative assistant, and possibly read by others in addition to the final recipient. Finally, sending your resume cold without a prior contact should only be a small part of your job search strategy, as the cost of mailing can add up.

## J.      Organizing Your Leads

Targeted follow-up is a key component of a successful job search, and it is a corollary to interviewing well and keeping the process afloat. In sales-oriented roles, if you are not persistent enough to follow up on a role, the employer may determine that you will not be persistent when following up *their leads* and therefore disqualify you. For other candidates, follow-up is important to stay front-of-mind regarding the role for which you have applied and also be the first candidate they consider (if qualified) for any new role that may open up.

> *Most networking efforts fail due to lack of consistent follow-up.*

The art of effective post-interview follow-up is discussed further in the last chapter of this book (After the Interview), so if you are at that stage, please turn to it now. In this chapter on networking, I want to make sure you are focused on the importance of organizing your job search leads, so that you have this information at your fingertips when you step into an interview and again when you are ready to follow up.

Getting organized on the networking front means knowing with whom you are connecting, why and other important data points, so that you can recall them when needed. It is easy to keep three job targets in your head. 30 are not so easy. You may think that you will remember information about the company, your value proposition for a particular role and other factors, but without this information at your fingertips, you are likely to miss something.

While it may seem like extra work to keep track of this information, if it seems like too much effort to keep track of what you are doing, you are probably "doing too much" on the networking front (i.e., connecting with too many contacts without slowing down to think about whether the connection makes sense).

> *It is much more productive to be thoughtful about your networking efforts than try to network like a maniac until something sticks.*

I often suggest to my clients that they arrange their job search and interview information in a chart form (such as in Microsoft Excel), with the headings of each column as follows. Here is an example of how to arrange it, with the **bolded** information sorted by columns and the specific data populating each row.

Spreadsheet #1 – Target Roles (with examples)

- **Contact at Target** – Jorge Rodriguez
- **Target Company Name** – Blankman & Co.
- **Nature of Relationship** – our kids play soccer together
- **What I Offer this Target** – my blend of technology and people skills plus large and small company expertise; they are growing quickly; looking for new COO; want someone decisive; my leadership roles and recruiting are a plus; they like that I have some sales background and can relate to sales team
- **Date/Stage of Last Contact** – email on 6/1
- **Next Steps** – follow up with phone call if haven't heard by 6/15
- **Notes** – also knows my good friend Ralph and probably Sara, need to bring this up somehow

Spreadsheet #2 – Connectors (with examples)

- **Name** – Lana Kinderman
- **Company Name** – Kinderman & Associates
- **Nature of Relationship** – known since graduate school
- **Reason for Connection** – will refer me to an UN jobs or others where she has contacts; said I may need to first apply, then she will forward resume to right people
- **Date/Point of Last Contact** – lunch on 5/10
- **Next Steps** – invite her to September networking event; finalize resume to send her
- **Notes** – remind Lana I am fluent in Spanish next time I see her

For the second spreadsheet, "Connectors" are people who are well poised to connect you to possible targets, and the "Reason for Connection" relates to the type of roles with which or individuals with whom they can connect you. For example, the Reason for Connection may be that the individual knows a number of private company CEOs or has other contacts in a certain field and is willing and able to help you connect with them (i.e., has a strong network and wants to support your job search by helping you make connections). Recruiters can also go on the Connectors chart, or a separate chart, since they also have the potential to connect you with a number of roles.

If you are applying to very different sets of roles (e.g., non-profit administration roles and corporate social responsibility (CSR) positions), I would suggest using additional sets of spreadsheets, or different workbooks within Excel if you find that easier, for each leg of your job search, naming them appropriately. The more structured you can make your approach, without complicating it, the better. (And if you find Excel intimidating, tables in Word also work. The point is to use this information to serve your job search, not to be tied to a certain format.)

Some of my clients prefer to include contact information in this same chart, although I generally keep it "clean," so that the spreadsheet is readable on an 8 ½ x 11 page. If there is too much information, it can turn into an unwieldy (and therefore unused) document.

Alternatively, you can record your job leads and next steps online, rather than through a spreadsheet. This is entirely in the best interest of the job seeker rather than an issue of best practice. I like to see everything on a few pages, neatly organized, and do not want to have to sign in and remember passwords to access my information. Others may appreciate the support of a system. Jibberjobber.com works well for many candidates, for example, and it is free (at the time of this printing) for a basic account.

My biggest challenges to getting my leads organized are:

_____

_____

I can address those challenges by:

_____

_____

## K.    New Graduates

A quick note to new graduates would be helpful here. If you are looking for your first "real" job after school, and you feel that you don't have a network yet, you may not be looking hard enough. Friends and business associates of relatives, professors, school administrators, religious leaders, former internship contacts and alumni (of all graduation years) are all part of your network. Reach out to them as appropriate, and keep the relationships alive over your career by keeping in touch. Finally, as I mentioned above, don't just ask what they can do for you over the short term but find ways to offer value in return.

As a senior financial advisor mentioned to me recently:

> *"As a student or new graduate, you think that if you do well in school or on tests, the world will come to reward you. That is not the way the world works. You need to get out there and make it happen for yourself."*

While none of your direct contacts may have a job for you, some of them may have further connections that can be helpful. In addition, your own friends and fellow students are your core network, and you can help each other along the way. These connections will only grow more valuable during the years to come.

Networking connections for me to create and maintain:

_____

_____

_____

# CHAPTER 4
# INTERVIEW STRATEGIES AND YOUR GAME PLAN

So how exactly should you approach the interview process? Is it more of a conversation or an interrogation? While some interviewees might profess (in jest or seriousness) that an interview is always the latter, it's actually a bit of both.

I strongly prefer to think of interviews as *very-pointed conversations*, rather than interrogations. If you are expecting the Spanish inquisition, you just may get it, but more out of exasperation on the part of the interviewer than as a methodological approach.

Interrogation <- - - - - - - - - - - - - - - - - - - - - - - - - - - - - -> Conversation

If you *do* happen to come across an interviewer who treats the meeting like an interrogation, you may try to see if you can turn it around. In fact, your goal in any interview is to keep it in the conversation zone, as colleagues discussing a matter of mutual interest. If not, and he/she is someone you would be working with closely, make sure to have a number of follow up meetings to see if the interviewer has mellowed since your first meeting.

Often you do not need to get every answer "right" in a barrage of questions (although it helps not to have any "wrong" answers either). Instead, your objective in the interview is to give helpful insights, ask interesting questions and move the conversation along to include the speaking points that you have brought to the table.

Never lose sight of the fact that you are talking to another person who has preferences, dislikes, blind spots, shortcomings and the like. He/she may have just returned from a snorkeling trip in Cancun, may be preoccupied with a sick child or parent at home or may be in the middle of a stressful conversation with his/her own boss about the profile of the candidate they are seeking as a hire or even whether the interviewer him/herself will continue with the company.

In other words, the interviewer has a life and his/her own joys, professional challenges, stressors and the like. Given that you are *talking to a person*, the best interviews flow like "real" conversations, with a highly professional bent and a few significant exceptions to your average cocktail talk, of course, as follows:

## A.     Overview of the Interview Process

1)  Every interview question has within it another underlying question, as I made abundantly clear in Chapter 2. As a reminder, what's the question?

*Why should I hire you?*

2)  The interview is not about what *you want*, it's about what *the employer needs*.

In short, an employer wants to hire you if you can solve whatever problems are presented in its business (sometimes called its "pain points," although not all interviewers are familiar with this term). **Talk about your value proposition in the context of the benefits you can bring to the employer.**

If you approach the interview as an opportunity to emphasize why the job will be a good career move for you, what you would like to get out of the role or why you think the company would be a great place for you to work, I can venture to say that you can kiss your chances of a callback goodbye. Why? Your interviewers already know that you are there because you think it may be a good move for your career, but they are honestly not (at that point) invested in your career, they are invested in the company (and their own careers, I might add). The better approach is to talk about what you can do for the team, department and company more generally, not what having the job will do for you.

### *In My Experience: Talk About Their Needs, Not Yours*

*In a number of interviews, when I have asked the question about why a candidate wanted to work at my company, one of their reasons was to shorten their commute to the office.*

*Sometimes, this was given as an afterthought, after a thoughtful response of substantive reasons. "And having a shorter commute is never a bad thing." Those responses succeeded, because they gave a nod to the practical realities of the situation and put the job seeker's need in perspective.*

*Other times, candidates would give me plain vanilla answers (i.e., ones that indicated no original thought) and emphasize that the long commute was killing them. Those responses failed, and I tuned out after that. I don't want to hear how bad you have it. I asked why you want to work for us? What if we move or you move, will you still be interested?*

*Your commute may be a driving force, but if you make that evident to your interviewer, be ready to keep driving.*

In the same way, if asked about why you are leaving (or left) your last job, the best answer is to discuss what you are looking for in a context of what is offered by the new employer (e.g., greater opportunity for collaboration). This is not about your needs; it is about your fit with the employer, which is an entirely different conversation.

3)   You do not take interviews to make friends.

While it is great to have friends at the office, and it certainly makes for a happier workplace, at no point during the interview process should you view anyone in human resources or the interviewing team as a potential friend. Even if you find that you have a sibling, cousin or best friend in common with an interviewer, or if you know each other from another part of your life, remember that *business is business.*

If you offer too much personal information, you may be viewed as unprofessional, whether or not the person would be happy to grab a coffee or drink with you one day outside the office. In addition, if you tell your "friend" interviewer your true concerns about a target job, your current role or anything else that is inconsistent with the answers you give to other interviewers along the process, you are putting him/her in a situation that presents an inherent conflict of interest.

Many times, the interviewer will either feel compelled to betray your confidence or otherwise sabotage your candidacy, because he/she is concerned about bringing you aboard based on the information you have shared. If he/she does keep your confidence and bring you aboard, resentment can also build if the match does not work out.

Finally, some interviewers intentionally build a rapport with candidates to see if they can get "the true story" out of them. Be on guard at all times, or as I always say to my clients, **"Be authentic but not transparent."**

*Note: If you are compelled to share something with only one or more members of the team, because it is a point that you need vetted but do not want widely disclosed, my best advice is to wait until you have an offer, unless the timing or circumstances dictate otherwise.*

You may be wondering how an interview can resemble a "true" conversation if the above points are also true. Yet, in fact, every human interaction involving words is a conversation, and the better you can connect with your interviewer, the more likely you are to get the job.

*So what is the secret of interviewing?* Focus on your objective: figure out what they are looking for in a candidate and present your candidacy in the best light.

You CANNOT control whether you get the job. There are many factors that have nothing to do with you. An internal candidate may already be a shoe-in. Another person interviewing for the same role may have a personal connection and more direct experience. Your interviewer may be turned off by something you say or having a bad day and unable to connect. You have to let go of whatever you cannot change and simply focus on your candidacy.

Preparation is key. Not repetition, but targeted preparation.

## B.    Your Game Plan for the Interview

Here is some overall guidance in formulating your game plan, which will be expanded in later chapters:

1) *Anticipate Questions* – be prepared for whatever may come

2) *Know and State Your Value* – determine what you bring to the table and how to communicate it clearly and succinctly, focusing on the top 3-5 points you want to convey

3) *Tailor Your Approach* – have a specific presentation for each employer and pay attention to clues in the job description, interview and elsewhere that may indicate their needs

4) *Know Yourself, Know the Employer and Know Your Resume* – show up as a candidate who has "done the homework"

5)  *Let Go of Outcomes* – despite your best efforts, you cannot anticipate everything or be "all things to all people;" there is always another interview

6)  *Don't Discuss Compensation or Benefits* – the only benefits you should discuss (in your first interview, at least) are the ones you bring

7)  *Close the Deal* – if you are genuinely interested, let the interviewer know it, and ask what are next steps and if/how you should proactively follow up; then follow up with a thank-you note within 24 hours

My tentative game plan for interview day:

_____

_____

_____

_____

Questions I have to finalize my game plan:

_____

_____

_____

_____

What I can do to get those questions answered:

_____

_____

_____

_____

# PART 2:

# YOUR VALUE PROPOSITION

# CHAPTER 5
# YOUR PERSONAL VALUE PROPOSITION

*Life can only be understood backwards, but it must be lived forwards.*
- Kierkegaard

Heading to an interview without having your value proposition front of mind is like hopping on a city bus without having the proper fare in hand. You may be fortunate to fish some coins (gems) out of the bottom of your backpack, but chances are that you'll be kicked off at the next stop.

In the four chapters in this Part 2 of the workbook, we will define your value proposition in four different ways. Roughly, these are as follows:

-   your general value proposition, including accomplishments,

-   your high-level and job-specific competencies,

-   your edge, and

-   your proposed solutions (i.e., benefits) for the employer and examples of where you have added value in the past.

We will start with the basics, such as what a "personal value proposition" actually means. Feel free to skip ahead and or use this workbook in any way that is most effective for you given the time and energy you have available to devote to this part of your interview preparation. For example, *if you have an interview in the next few days,* you may wish to start with the open-ended exercises in this chapter and then skip to your proposed solutions for the employer in Chapter 8.

If either of the following is true:

-   you are reading this book at a point that you are in a crossroads or inflection point (i.e., stage of significant growth) career-wise, or

-   you have never before tried to define the value that you bring in an employment context,

then you will want to work through all of the exercises and think about your value proposition from an open-ended, comprehensive and long-term approach. In other words, try each of the different approaches until you can define an overarching vision for yourself rather than jumping right into what an employer needs (which could certainly get you a job, but not necessarily one that works for you).

As one executive – who has been on interviews many times himself over a twenty-year career and has hired a number of new employees for teams he has lead and managed – said when he read an early draft of this book:

> *"If you don't take time to understand your value proposition in terms of where you want to take your career over the long term, you may have the right fare, but you could be on the wrong bus."*

For the workbook portion of this chapter, I suggest you do this in a place most conducive to open, honest thinking, whether that is a quiet place in your home or a stimulating environment such as a coffee shop – whatever works to get your best results.

## A.      What Is a Value Proposition?

If you are not already familiar with the concept of a *personal value proposition*, congratulations on the discovery. Learning what it is and applying it to your career decisions is well worth the cost of this book and will serve you for many years to come.

Let's start with the idea of value propositions generally. We all instinctively appreciate the intrinsic value propositions of various companies, for example. If I asked you what value a grocery store, movie theater or cell phone provider added to people's lives, you would easily be able to tell me and distinguish the value of one type of company's offering from another. At their most basic level, grocery stores provide food and related products for sale; movie theaters show recent or classic movies to groups of audiences on big screens and cell phone providers allow us to use phones without being tied to our homes or other centralized locations.

In the case of grocery stores, you probably could also tell me why you might drive to one that is five or ten miles from your home rather than a store located closer to you. *What would compel you to drive further for groceries?* The second store may have more selection, fresher fruit or better prices. It may be easier to navigate, with a better parking lot, and the cashiers may be friendlier. Alternatively, the store that is further away could have only a few or none of these advantages but offer the particular type of coffee, yogurt or fish that you prefer to buy, and you may wish to consolidate your shopping into one trip. In other words, while grocery stores offer many of the same products and the same overall service proposition to their customers, they are not commodities. Instead, they have individual advantages and disadvantages (those above and others) that we can recognize and discuss.

## B.      What Is a Personal Value Proposition?

At a basic level, your personal value proposition operates the same way as a company's would, and employers operate like your customers. Just as people need food, water, shelter and good wifi (so my children tell me), employers have various needs as well. In a commercial context, for example, a company needs employees who add value in the following ways and CEOs and other C-level officers, partners, managing directors, executive directors, senior managers, vice presidents and others who can think, execute and manage across all or multiple areas below:

1. envision, create, market and/or support its products or services,

2. provide strategic guidance to the organization,

3. create value through expansion, partnerships and other means,

4. keep it on track financially and manage its business risks,

5. help it stay (or get) out of trouble,

6. run and monitor its systems,

7. recruit, train and/or manage its employees,

8. maintain and expand its office space and/or operations, and

9. serve other needs of the organization.

Regardless of your specific problem-solving abilities, your role at an organization falls into one or more of the above categories. Forget about your job title for a moment, and focus on which of these basic needs (one or more) that you are serving. You will have the opportunity in Chapter 8 to take a more literal, organized approach and to tailor your value proposition to the needs of your target role.

## C.    How Your Value Proposition Relates to Your Personal Brand

Your value proposition is an important part of your personal brand, but it is not your entire brand. Your brand includes every aspect of how you present yourself personally and professionally, from how you speak (including choice of vocabulary) to where and whether you choose to speak (i.e., which public speaking engagements, if any, you seek out and accept). It includes whom you accept into your inner circle, and whether you appear collaborative, humorous, hard-driving or bookish or exhibit a whole range of other traits.

In other words, our brand is the image we present to the world. In the best scenario, it is an extension of who we really are, albeit the best version of ourselves. This is true whether you are an artist or an accountant. If you are not comfortable with the value proposition that you create on these pages but long to *be* someone or something else, it is in your power to change it, just as you can change your brand to be more authentic (which takes so much less work to maintain).

As you create your value proposition, you also create how you talk about yourself. As Michael Melcher wrote in *The Creative Lawyer*, your core communications tool is your positioning statement about who you are and what you want (the key messages about you). In particular, he wrote:

> *"Good communication begins with self-awareness about who you are and what you want in life. The main work in communications preparation isn't anticipating what others will think of you – it's taking time to figure out what you think of you."*

## D.    An Open-Ended Approach to Value Proposition

*(Note: If you have the time, I suggest you complete this worksheet "cold" before turning to the next chapter, unless you need help generating ideas.)*

I serve one or more of the following basic employer needs:

_____

_____

If I were asked about my "strengths," I would list the following:

_____

_____

_____

_____

The technical skills I bring are:

_____

_____

_____

My role fits into the organization's big picture by:

_____

_____

_____

I have already delivered similar value in other roles (list specific examples), such as the following:

1) _____

_____

2) _____

_____

3) _____

_____

4) _____

_____

My target role(s) would specifically require me to:

_____

_____

_____

I will do a great job fulfilling those needs because:

_____

_____

_____

If some of my value proposition for this role comes from outside of the employment context, such as volunteer work, I have added value in the past by:

_____

_____

_____

If this new role has aspects that I have not yet performed in other roles, my transferable skills and talents that prepare me for the challenge include:

_____

_____

_____

Distinguishing myself from others who might have more, less or similar experience, I am a better hire because:

_____

_____

_____

I consistently receive positive feedback that I:

_____

_____

## E.   Summing Up

My "elevator pitch" of who I am is:

_____

_____

My highest value proposition overall (i.e., where I excel) is:

_____

_____

_____

The tailored value I can deliver to this target employer (i.e., specific problem-solving for its most pressing needs) is:

_____

_____

_____

Problems I have solved for other employers (see above for reference) include:

1) _____

_____

2) _____

_____

3) _____

_____

My vision for the company, department and/or role is:

1) _____

_____

2) _____

_____

3) _____

_____

# CHAPTER 6
# CORE COMPETENCIES THAT GET YOU HIRED

What interviewers want most, almost invariably, is to find the right candidate and get back to work. Under normal circumstances, they have no incentive to drag out the process and would much rather being doing something else (sometimes anything other than) conducting interviews, vetting candidates and making offers to new employees. This is especially true if their department has had significant turnover, a key person has left or is planning to retire or they are in a hiring spree. The quicker they can come to a sound conclusion, the better.

How can you demonstrate that you are the one to hire, so you can get the job and both you and the interviewer (soon-to-be colleague) can get to work? It depends on the type of role, field, seniority and criteria of your interviewer, as well as what you determine is the best "argument" for you as a candidate. In some cases and interview contexts, your competencies are front and center. This chapter helps you prepare for a competencies-based interview and be ready to address your competencies in any other interview format.

## A.    Your Strategy to Get Hired

The four chapters in the Value Proposition portion of this book represent different ways to get at the heart of this multi-faceted issue: why should an employer hire *you*? In this chapter, we focus on the qualities, competencies and skills that you can demonstrate to show that you have the requisite bundle of "stuff" that interviewers are seeking from their next hire. Some competencies are more valued in some fields than others (such as creativity and innovation), while others (such as leadership ability) can apply to just about any job at any level. More general skills, which are often also high-level skills, are also called "transferable skills" because they can be transferred from one field to another.

*Real-Life Example*

*I mention above that leadership ability applies to just about any job at any level. Where have I seen examples of this assertion? If I look back to my high school summer days working at a Mexican-style restaurant in my hometown, it was immediately clear to anyone paying attention which of the full-time staff would rise to management (with greater compensation and, probably, job satisfaction) and which employees would continue to spend their days whipping up burritos and nacho combos. It was a cast of characters, from the day manager Lois who was fond of saying "less leaning, more cleaning" and did her best to run a fun but tight ship to Eddie who shoved a taco in his pocket every chance he thought no one was looking (and whom Lois eventually fired). Leadership at its most basic level includes drive, initiative and the ability to inspire others, and this runs across roles.*

*There are, of course, jobs at which true leadership is not rewarded. These include roles at organizations that are truly dysfunctional, from a company with an egomaniac (or team of them) running the show, who is/are jealous of anyone else's success, to an obviously inefficient organization, where it seems that no one has given any thought to whom they are serving and why, such as the DMV (so cunningly embellished in the movie Zootopia).*

In Chapter 5, you had the opportunity to work through an open-ended value proposition, based on your own thoughts and without a top-down framework. I ordered the chapters in this manner so that you do not get "boxed in" to a certain approach to thinking about value proposition but instead can first get some of your ideas down on paper.

This Chapter 6 functions as (1) an idea-generator for these high-level, transferable qualities and skills and, later in the chapter, job-specific skills, that you may possess but have not thought about in the context of interviewing and (2) a lexicon (vocabulary) that serves as a means to structure (organize) your thoughts about your strengths and any gaps.

Note for the very literal reader, I do not suggest that you communicate your skills in the manner set forth below without being artful about it. For example, if your interviewer asks you to "tell me about yourself," don't launch into a list of "well, I have big picture vision, good presentation skills, a strong work ethic and…" As I said in Chapter 2 when discussing the interviewer's and job seeker's dilemmas, the quickest way to get to an answer is not always the most effective one.

In Chapter 7, we work through your unique "edge" that differentiates you from other candidates, whether gained from your career or other life experiences. In Chapter 8 we bring it all together, discussing solutions that you can bring to the target employer and the professional accomplishments you can present to demonstrate your ability to deliver those solutions.

With your value proposition fully vetted and tailored to the specific employer, in Chapter 9, we move to that capstone interview question of *"Why do you want to work here?"* If you have felt in prior interviews that you had nothing or little of value to say when asked this question, you will be brave and confident with your value proposition and due diligence completed, as you will know what you can offer to the company, what problems you can solve for them and why you are the person to solve them.

**To prepare for an interview that is coming up very soon** – i.e., in the next week or less – I might skip to Chapter 8 at this point, as it offers most expeditious way to arrive at what is essentially a job-centered value proposition, rather than the more comprehensive exploration of your overall value and how it relates to one or more potential roles and jobs. I mention this because it is easy to get overwhelmed under pressure, and your talking points need to be very clear and concise. If you have a bit more time, but still not enough time to work through all of Chapters 5 through 7, you may wish to start with the open-ended questions about value proposition in Chapter 5.

**If you have the time, to be *fully prepared* for your interviews,** I suggest you work through all of these angles, since you never know until you walk into the room what type of interview you will face. In the end, you might find that you are a stronger candidate by one measure than another, and certainly it pays to speak to your strengths by subtly moving the conversation toward your greatest value-add to the employer.

While job seekers often feel that an interviewer *should* be taking an expansive view of them as candidates, the reality is that every interview includes some degree of box-checking (especially in junior roles). Data-driven interviewers, or ones who operate in that environment, may focus on this more than others, and for some roles it makes sense for one's skillset to be a driving criteria (as long as it is not the only one). In addition, sometimes interviewers become box-checkers to a greater degree if they know that their emotions have gotten the better of them in the past, hiring a candidate with whom they "clicked" and though they could teach the relevant skills, only to get burned later.

While the next page has a list of qualities, I cannot emphasize strongly enough that getting your next (or ideal) job is *not* simply about being able to check off that you have mastered certain competencies. It's about delivering value, and the skillsets are simply a more measurable proxy for the value you can deliver.

## B.   High-Level Competencies

Here's a list of 36 high-level competencies and traits, many of which are valued across a wide range of roles, in fields as diverse as product development, strategic development, sales, marketing, finance, audit, research, creative/design, engineering, information technology, human resources, law, compliance, education and administration (and a whole lot more could be added to this list).  At this point, I suggest that you take some initial notes about your reaction to this list. Are there some skills that pop out at you as ones that are:

- sought after in your field,

- needed by a specific target employer (if you have one identified),

- strengths,

- gaps, and/or

- especially for career changers or more junior professionals, skills you have or want to develop that are underutilized in your current role?

As you review the competencies on the next page, keep in mind that you should look over the course of your career as a whole, not only what you have done in your most recent role. I lost track of Lois (from my example above) in the years that followed, but if she later obtained a role that was not overtly geared toward leadership (e.g., starting as a bookkeeper or junior data analyst), she would nonetheless retain her leadership ability as a core competency and could incorporate those skills as she progressed in her new field.

*Side note:* We often recognize our own frustration when we are expected to exhibit skills we *don't* have but do not realize (or downplay) how it is equally frustrating to be limited in our ability to use skills we *do* have, especially if we see others in roles that we think we could do better. Over time, we discount our ability to use our skills, and they go unrecognized. This is your chance to unearth them.

| | |
|---|---|
| *Big Picture Vision* | *Design/Visual Communication* |
| *Strategic Thinking* | *Collaboration/Team Player* |
| *Strategic Planning* | *Entrepreneurial Skills* |
| *Innovation/Creativity/Curiosity* | *Comfort with Risk* |
| *Resilience* | *Influence/Political Capital* |
| *Grit* | *Marketing/Sales Ability* |
| *Board/Stakeholder Management* | *Achieving Results on Deadline* |
| *Leadership/Mentoring Ability* | *Decisiveness* |
| *Industry Knowledge* | *Pragmatism* |
| *Customer-Service Orientation* | *"Tough Skin"* |
| *Grasp of P&L/Financial Analysis* | *Sense of Humor* |
| *Project Management* | *Diplomacy/Restraint* |
| *Organization/Ability to Provide Structure* | *Clear Head/Calm/Groundedness* |
| *Risk-Management* | *Work Ethic* |
| *Negotiation Skills* | *Credibility* |
| *Oral Communication* | *Integrity* |
| *Writing Skills* | *Judgment/Discernment* |
| *Research* | *Motivation of Self and Others* |

While I cannot say that the above list holds the totality of skills needed or that it ever would – that would be both ignorance and hubris – it is what I would call a *very good start*.

*Additional skills (if any):*

_____

You can make additional notes on the following pages of your top skills and examples of when you have exhibited such skills. Do not forget to frame the examples in terms of accomplishments that will be relevant for your target employers. Additional copies are available at www.annemariesegal.com. (Click on "Worksheets.")

*Skill #1:* _____

*Is it highly valued in my target roles?* ____ *yes*    ____ *no*    ____ *not sure*

Top Accomplishments That Demonstrate This Skill

*Example 1:*

_____

_____

*Example 2:*

_____

_____

*Example 3:*

_____

_____

*Skill #2:* _____

*Is it highly valued in my target roles?* ____ *yes*    ____ *no*    ____ *not sure*

Top Accomplishments That Demonstrate This Skill

*Example 1:*

_____

_____

*Example 2:*

_____

_____

*Example 3:*

_____

_____

*Skill #3:* _____

*Is it highly valued in my target roles?* ____ *yes*   ____ *no*   ____ *not sure*

Top Accomplishments That Demonstrate This Skill

*Example 1:*

_____

_____

*Example 2:*

_____

_____

*Example 3:*

_____

_____

*Skill #4:* _____

*Is it highly valued in my target roles?* ____ *yes*   ____ *no*   ____ *not sure*

Top Accomplishments That Demonstrate This Skill

*Example 1:*

_____

_____

*Example 2:*

_____

_____

*Example 3:*

_____

_____

Top Skills that are Needed or Helpful in my Target Roles (that I do not possess or need to improve):

*Skill:* _____

My Plans to Address this Gap

_____

_____

_____

*Skill:* _____

My Plans to Address This Gap

_____

_____

_____

For Career Changers (and Junior Candidates), Skills I Have or Want to Develop that Are Not Emphasized or Required in My Current Roles:

_____

_____

_____

My Plans to Find the Right Role or Develop these Skills

_____

_____

_____

Additional Notes

_____

_____

Congratulations! You are on your way to a successful interview.

## C.    Some More Thoughts About Skills

While I refer off-handedly to "box-checking" in the text above, these high-level skills are not categories that can be objectively measured. There is diversity within each of the skills and how they can manifest in certain candidates, as well as how they can be applied in various roles. In fact, a whole chapter (or book) could be written about each skill, and some competencies in the could be further bifurcated – e.g., someone could take on numerous leadership roles but not be an effective mentor, could be great at cross-functional collaboration but not work well on day-to-day team matters or may know how to put together a PowerPoint slide deck that conveys ideas through visual means (visual communication) but not be artistically inclined or able to "design" in other contexts.

Another point worth noting here is that while a certain company or role may *benefit* from a certain set of skills does not mean that the company *values* that skill. To use law firms as an example, collaboration skills may be discussed as goals of the firm during partner meetings, corporate retreats, or in other contexts, but whether a firm actually seeks and rewards attorneys who are truly collaborative in their practices is dependent on the structure and values of the individual firm, and many value individual contributions much more highly than collaborative efforts. On the other hand, at the partner level business development is often a key skill, and a proven book of business is often needed to make a lateral move across firms, at least in most practice areas and markets.

Yet even in this case, there are exceptions, such as in the "white shoe" law firms at which partners and associates team together to serve a limited number of longstanding, high-profile institutions (that bring in major recurring revenue) rather than independently develop a wider range of mid-market or smaller clients. At those top, old-line firms, to join at the partner level a candidate essentially needs to demonstrate a proven flair for servicing these specialized client relationships, with a strong pedigree to boot. Bringing in new clients would create additional value for the firm and specifically benefit the individual partner who generated them, of course, but only if the additional client relationships fit the firm's business model and do not present conflicts of interest to existing clients.

For law firm associates, business development may be valued by a firm, in theory or in practice, but "work ethic" (tolerance for working long, erratic hours) and being a "good lawyer" (problem-solving skills and substantive competence) often trump an aptitude for bringing in new clients, unless a substantial book of business has already been built. Of course, this varies among individual firms, and some firms pride themselves on client service as well as mentoring and growth of younger lawyers.

## D.    Role-Specific Competencies and Skills

Now that you have identified your overarching transferable skills, you can turn your attention more concrete skills that are specific to a certain field or role. Interviewers are often looking for very specific competencies and skills, although as noted above, they may hire someone who has the aptitude to develop those competencies and/or skills if they can come across as more impressive overall than those who possess them already.

Role-specific competencies and skills are even more specific for the actual job for which you are applying, although there may be strong overlap among similar roles. As I discuss further in Chapter 8, often the best way to understand what competencies would be required for a specific role is to start with the job description and then compare it to other job descriptions for similar roles. Notice what changes and what remains constant among the descriptions.

Here are functional competencies that may be needed as a recruiter:

*Examples of Specific Competencies for Recruiting*

*Hiring Criteria Assessments*                     *Career Assessments*

*Role Definition (with client)*                   *Resume Review*

*Candidate Interviews*                            *Expectation Management*

*Candidate Evaluations*                           *Job Description Review*

*Job Search Strategies*                           *Employee Relocations*

As I mentioned above, these categories are not complete – this example functions more as an illustration and idea-generator than a catch-all – as these abilities are clearly not the only ones that a recruiter might need to possess, and in some cases he/she may not possess or use all of the above skills. In fact, one of the struggles for many candidates is that they have been pigeon-holed into a few areas rather than given an opportunity to develop a wider range of skills, which is part of the reason this exercise is so helpful (as it gives job candidates a better view of where their gaps or blind spots may be). As you will see further in Chapter 8, certain of these skills may be more or less important in a specific job, due to (among other reasons) specific client needs, how the firm or department is oriented, and what skills are missing to round out the existing team.

Here is another example, in this case of how you might frame a range of specific competencies for an employment lawyer:

*Examples of Specific Competencies for Employment Law*

*Advising/Counseling Clients*                     *Interacting with Regulators*

*Drafting Motions and Briefs*                      *Investigating Complaints*

*Appearing in Court*                              *Negotiating Terms/Agreements*

*Depositions and Discovery*                        *Drafting Agreements*

*Conducting Trainings*                            *Conducting Legal Research*

*For attorneys and those in certain other fields, it may help in addition to be ready to discuss the substantive, practice-oriented competencies that the individual has.*

## Substantive Legal Areas

| | |
|---|---|
| *Labor/Employment Litigation* | *EEOC/Equal Rights* |
| *Mediations/Settlements* | *Discrimination* |
| *Workplace Investigations* | *Worker's Compensation* |
| *DOL Audits/Regulations* | *WARN Issues* |
| *Noncompetition and Severance* | *Work Visas/Immigration* |
| *Disciplines/Terminations* | *ERISA Compliance* |
| *FMLA/Accommodations* | *Policies and Procedures* |

If you would like to create your own list of specific competencies, you can do so here. I have given you some extra lines to experiment and come to a final conclusion.

Area of General Competency:

_____

Substantive/Technical/Core Competencies:

_____

_____

_____

_____

_____

_____

_____

_____

_____

## E.      Rolling It Up and Communicating Your Value

As a job candidate, your goal is not necessarily to have the broadest range of competencies and skills that could possibly be applicable to your target role, although sometimes it helps to demonstrate well-developed critical thinking in your general area of expertise, but find a match between your strongest skills and the needs of your target role(s). Your next task is to be able to communicate your value to the employer, which for many working professionals involves not only defining "what they do" but also how to group it into categories and discuss it intelligently. As I say often to my clients, when you communicate your value, you need to do two things: (1) differentiate yourself from other candidates and (2) "roll up" the specific details of your value proposition into an easily digestible presentation.

For example, the prominent data scientist Drew Conway has boiled down the core competencies in data science to a Venn diagram of:

- hacking skills,

- math/stats knowledge, and

- substantive [i.e., business] expertise

with each set of skills keeping the other in check.

Others have added communication as a fourth key skill, which as we have discussed above is a critical competency across many fields (and not specific to the field of data science, of course).  I concur with this addition, as I have seen first-hand across a range of technical fields that if a candidate has all of the hard skills required in a role but cannot communicate well to non-technical management and employees across the company, this generally deters the candidate from gaining any real traction and advancement in their field. For international candidates who are working in a non-native language – especially one that is very different from what they learned as a child – this may prompt some self-reflection about whether speech/diction or other classes that can improve English (or another relevant) language presentation is highest priority for their continued career training, even above other skills that could be acquired. For native English speakers who "speak geek" but have trouble relating to people outside of their field, they may gain more utility from simply practicing with the right audience or working with a coach who can help them translate from "science or engineering speak" (or "legalese", etc.) to "plain English."

From an interviewer's perspective, a short list like the one above could be used to evaluate a candidate with respect to each of these areas and get a sense of the person as a whole. A job seeker, on the other hand, could seek to direct a conversation around these core competencies, in order to give structure to the presentation of his/her value proposition.

This top-down view of your value proposition is available to any candidate, regardless of whether your current job operates in a very narrow space or pulls you in 50 different directions on any given day. I was recently working with a C-level administrative assistant and office manager (let's call her Beth), for example, to formulate her value proposition based on her core competencies. We discussed the various range of roles that could be open to Beth next, from compliance to a finance-related role (as she currently provides support to both the CFO and the head of the firm), and how Beth's value proposition can and should change for each potential target, as she can slice and dice her current list of responsibilities in a number of different ways. I gave Beth the following overview of how she may structure a presentation, picking and choosing those parts that make sense for an individual interview. The main idea is to structure her response so that she covers each major aspect of her current position:

*I would love to hear more about the expectations of this role, because I can probably give a more helpful response with that in mind. In the meantime, I will tell you about my current position and the value I add there. My role essentially spans three categories: relationship-management, the organization of "things" (for lack of a better word) and my individual workload.*

*First, I work very closely with the owners of the firm and coordinate across different departments to make sure their priorities are met. As you can imagine, this involves managing a lot of different personalities and making sure things get done even if I don't have the direct authority to make it happen. Priorities can sometimes shift as well, so I need to roll with that and make sure the team does too. The best, and frankly the worst, part of this aspect of my job [said with a laugh or smile] is that I never know what my day is going to look like, I only know that it is going to be interesting.*

The above communicates (to varying degrees) the following competencies:

leadership, customer-service orientation, negotiation, oral communication, collaboration, comfort with risk, resilience, "tough skin," diplomacy, calm, influence, credibility, integrity, judgment and motivation of others.

*Second, I spend a lot of my day making sure that schedules, information, files and the office space generally are organized and running efficiently. This can range from setting the calendar for securities filings to something as simple as making sure that a keycard is programmed for an employee's first day. I organize travel visas and flights, order furniture, manage the security staff…. The list goes on, and often these are things I have identified myself that need to get done. One key part of the organizational piece, of course, is to make sure that the owners stay on track with the deadlines we need to meet, without becoming a pest, and on occasion try to push (or negotiate) the deadlines if we can't meet them.*

This second part communicates the competencies of:

big picture vision and strategic planning (each to the extent she juggles priorities and essentially creates company policy in the absence of guidance), industry knowledge, project management, risk management, negotiation, oral communication, achieving results on deadline, decisiveness, pragmatism and self-motivation.

*Third, I have my own individual workload of course, as I mentioned. I process invoices and accounts payable. I review customer accounts to make sure everything is accurate and manage responses to customer complaints. I address compliance issues, particularly SEC compliance. I even deal with credit card fraud on occasion, and I have to say that I have learned more about that than I would ever want to know.*

This last piece communicates some of the competencies already mentioned above and also indicates financial knowledge and could indicate industry knowledge, sales ability and an ability to research (collectively needed to get to the bottom of and address complaints) as well as creativity, intellectual curiosity (possibly) and integrity in working with the credit card companies. In addition, as she discusses her dedication in all of these areas, work ethic is an implied skill.

This only leaves five of the 36 high-level competencies in the above list unaddressed: strategic thinking, writing skills, public speaking, design/visual communication and entrepreneurial skills, none of which are the top skills valued in an administrative role at this level (by most companies). If Beth wanted to market herself for a job needing those skills, of course, her narrative could be adapted to emphasize them.

I hope that the example above is illustrative for your situation as well. To make Beth's value proposition more manageable, we have broken it into three parts, which is easier to remember when she is on the spot in an interview. Structuring it this way also makes the information accessible to the interviewer, who may wish at any point to break in with questions for Beth (after which it is easy for them to pick up the conversation where it left off, since she can recall which of the three categories she was addressing at the time). Third, it encourages the interviewer to stay with Beth's story until the end, waiting for all three aspects of her current job to be fully described. Finally, since Beth started out her value proposition by stating that she wanted to hear more about the specific expectations of the target role, the perfect segue after this presentation is to ask which of these three aspects (of Beth's current job) the interviewer thinks would be most relevant to the new position.

This same formula can be used whether you design rockets or sell real estate for a living. You can break down your job into its component parts, discuss it at a high-level in a manner that reveals your competencies and provide enough detail to spike the interviewer's interest and differentiate yourself from other candidates.

As a final point here, do not forget that in the context of a specific interview – as we will discuss further in Chapter 8 – you will want to emphasize those categories of skills that you believe are most helpful to fill the target employer's needs. In the context of your career trajectory as a whole, however, the best way to craft a job search is to understand your strengths and interests first, and then look for potential jobs that either (1) embody those skills sets or (2) provide a bridge from where you are to the place you wish to take your career over the long term.

## F.    The "Gestalt" of a Job Candidate

As part of this discussion, I should further mention (and try not to blunder, as is often done) the concept of gestalt. In the famous phrase of the German gestalt psychologist, Kurt

Koffka, the whole is other than the sum of its parts (often incorrectly translated as "the whole is greater than the sum of its parts"). While I cannot do justice to gestaltism here, it is worth noting that while the above 36 skills are arguably the most valued by interviewers – some more than others depending on the job and the individual interviewer – as a candidate you also present a totality or "unified whole" that goes beyond any deconstruction into skillsets. This is why, for example, someone who has no industry experience or lacks what the job description lists as a critical skill may be chosen over candidates that seemed like a "shoe-in" to the position. The candidate presented a better overall package and competent (if not targeted) technical skills – and likely a vision and excitement about the role and what could be accomplished – and at the same time convinced the interviewer that whatever he/she was lacking could be easily learned. (Note: this is sometimes easier to communicate when addressing the hiring partner/manager directly, rather than a recruiter or human resource professional who is wary of presenting a candidate who does not fit the "requirements" or could be a risky hire.)

In fact, interviewers may prefer one candidate over another for reasons a totality of reasons ("they just strike me as a better fit"), and they might not be able vocalize their gut feeling and the fact that they wish to rally behind one candidate or eliminate another, but they are nonetheless certain about their reaction. Other times, they cannot communicate the specifics of their preference, but there is an underlying competency that tips the balance. If they took the energy to break it down further – and precious time they do not always have for every candidate, or may decide has little payoff for them in the long run if they have already eliminated someone – the objection might be a question of integrity ("there's just something I don't trust about the guy") or a feeling that someone is too entrepreneurial ("she wouldn't be happy here; she would be bored") or not entrepreneurial enough ("she would be out of her element; she would get eaten alive").

At the same time, interviewers may have a specific competence in mind, based on their overall needs for the group ("we need to get someone in here who can help sell our ideas to management") or a reaction to the person who was just terminated ("this time I need someone who can think for him/herself") and attempt to avoid the issues that arose with the last hire. Finally, while at this point we are discussing higher-level soft skills, the reason for the objection may be entirely clear ("she just doesn't have enough experience in X").

Sally Cordovano, Director of Business Development of W by Worth, said when she looks for new candidates, she needs to get a certain read on them in the interview:

> *"Since we are a clothing company, of course our candidates must have an appreciation of style and the difference that quality, versatile clothes can make in expressing oneself and developing a personal brand. Beyond that, I look for someone who is a 'people person' and can easily and naturally create relationships with potential clients. Third, although many of our candidates are looking for balance rather than a 40-hour work week – whether they are returning from raising children or downshifting from a corporate role – I need to make sure they understand that while I am offering a part-time job, it's still a real job. I look for candidates who have the work ethic to put in the time, care and creativity to build meaningful relationships with clients. Only if I see all three of these elements in a candidate do they make sense for us to hire."*

Perceived hiring needs for a role may differ among various parties in the hiring process (e.g., recruiting/HR, individual hiring managers, potential colleagues and others who may be interviewing you). Also, if you are working through a recruiter, that individual may or may not be privy to the inner workings of the organization and may even seek to get input from you in your debriefing ("what questions did they ask?") so he/she can help you decode and put forward your best presentation.

> *Do your interviewers give you any clues*
> *about their individual or collective agendas*
> *or what skills they need most at the moment?*

It is extremely important that you recognize these undercurrents exist, even if they are not communicated to you, because it helps you be attune to whether the interviewer gives any clues about what he/she is listening for in your presentation. A question that you might think is not important because it does not fit your perception of the interviewer's critical need may in fact be the pivotal one.

Do you remember, for example, my point above that business development skills are not as highly valued in law firm associates as in their partners? While this is often true in law and other professional service firms – since someone needs to be at the desk doing the work – there are some that take a longer view of their associates' futures and, in addition, business development skills may be one of a particular firm's highest values at that moment.

There could be a variety of reasons why a firm becomes focused on business development (i.e., getting new clients) above other needs. For example, it could be a young and growing firm, there could be an eye to business succession (which they may or may not make known) or a top rainmaker may have just left, causing the firm to scramble to keep associates busy (this latter factor may also cause the hiring process to come to a delay or halt in one or more practice areas or the firm as a whole, as they seek to replace the departing partner's income, especially if the firm does not have sufficient reserves and foresight to plan ahead for their next busy phase, has a cash crunch or is generally conservative in its finances).

To open your mind to possible qualities and skills that could be helpful in your target role, you may wish to hypothesize about what would be most important (and what hidden skills might be needed) across a variety of roles. For example, leadership is an obvious skill in certain roles but not emphasized (while nonetheless needed) in others.

**Take an expansive view. Sometimes, the further we step back, the more we see.**

Johnnie M. Jackson, Jr., former Vice President, General Counsel & Secretary, Olin Corporation (OLN:NYSE) offered this comment on what makes or breaks a General Counsel (or GC). You will see that it cuts across many of the competencies and traits discussed above:

> *"I would say that 'people skills' and knowledge of the organization and who 'gets things done' (and don't) are critical to any GC's effectiveness. GC's 'have influence' but not real 'power' within most organizations. The 'decisions' on most matters are made on the business side – so a GC has to be tuned in to how each decision-maker 'works and*

*thinks.' The GC often finds that he/she is in the role of a majority whip on the floor of congress, a champion for an idea or tactical strategy. Their legal skills and people skills are key components of their ability to help business decision-makers at all levels manage risks appropriately to a given situation, keep things simple and understandable (so important) and get things done on time every time."*

## G.     Note for Recent Graduates

If all (or most) of your life you have been a student, you may not have ever had the occasion or need to think about competencies or transferable skills, especially if you had a major that was more concerned with "teaching you to think" than getting you a job after school ended. Welcome to the real world, as they say, and the more expensive you get as your career progresses, the more clarity you will need to have on the value you add. One of the best descriptions that I have ever heard about this distinction is:

> *"When you are young, people value you because you are smart or talented. As you get older, people value you because you are useful."*

If you are fresh out of school, the distinction may make you bristle. If you are a senior candidate, business owner or frequent interviewer, you will nod your head in agreement and probably have even further wisdom to add to the phrase. While it is clearly an oversimplification, the kernel of truth is that if you are paid "X dollars" to do a job, the employer expects at least equal usefulness/value (if not much more) in return.

Notes from this chapter:

_____

_____

_____

_____

_____

# CHAPTER 7
# YOUR EDGE

In addition to the sought-after skills you possess, which we addressed in the last chapter, a highly effective interviewing strategy is to pinpoint and communicate your "edge" to an interviewer. Not every job candidate has an edge, but many of them do.

## A.  What's an Edge?

For the purpose of persuading someone you are the right person to hire (or promote) for a certain role, your edge is what differentiates you from other candidates. It is not a zero-sum game where some job seekers win and others lose. (Yes, only one can win each job, but the job market is more than a game of musical chairs.) We all have an edge, and you will be better able to present yourself for opportunities if you have greater insight into yours.

## B.  How Do You Get an Edge?

You have an edge if you possess a quality, skill or experience that is directly related to the position for which you are applying and will make you better able to succeed in the role.

Here are some examples:

- a COO candidate may be a former recruiter (and have a great eye for acquiring new talent) or may have lived abroad for a number of years before returning to the U.S. (and possess a deep understanding of how to create a diverse, international workforce);

- a financial advisor working with special needs families may have faced similar challenges as a parent or witnessed them through contact with a close friend's child (and be able to demonstrate compassion, relate to their experience and know how to create an effective financial plan);

- an architect or real estate developer may have a LEED certification and special interest in environmentally friendly construction; or

- a marketing officer may be an active participant personally in social media platforms such as Twitter or blogging (and understand how to achieve higher market penetration for the firm or organization's products and services).

Your experiences do not automatically give you an edge, but if you can learn from them, they will provide you relevant context for your jobs and help demonstrate that you have a capacity to solve a greater range and complexity of problems presented.

You can gain a different type of edge, of course, by leveraging relevant contacts within an organization, which may help you get the job. This type of "edge" has nothing to do with the intrinsic value of what you offer the company, unless it also allows you to get things done within the organization more quickly and effectively than the average candidate (see the skill of Influence/Political Capital in the chart in Chapter 6 above).

## C.      What Unique Value Do *You* Add?

Even if you don't feel you have a specific edge, you nonetheless have something that puts you ahead of others who are interviewing for the same role.

You may be evaluated among a sea of candidates with similar backgrounds (and possibly some who are very different from you). You are by no means a commodity, even if you are the most entry-level candidate.

Note: Your edge needs to be consistent with your brand. If your edge is that you are familiar with international markets and customs, for example, be current on the news in the cities and countries where the company operates. Know the customs and learn a few words in the relevant language(s).

### *How do you stand out?*

And not just stand out, but in a way that is marketable. And how can you make it part of your professional brand? Think about what *value you add* that is different than anyone else may possess who is applying for the same role for which you are interviewing. What specifically do you offer that is not simply a laundry list of the things that need to get done?

## D.      What's Your Edge?

What are your defining life events and professional experiences?

_____

_____

_____

What are your top professional and personal values?

_____

_____

_____

Do you have special skills that are unique? How might they relate to your field?

_____

_____

_____

What have you done in "past lives" (e.g., prior careers, travel or education) that could be helpful for your target role(s)?

_____

_____

_____

Do you have a unique "lens" on the world (that enhances your professional acumen)?

_____

_____

_____

What additional awareness do you have about your own edge?

_____

_____

_____

# CHAPTER 8
# YOUR JOB-SPECIFIC VALUE PROPOSITION AND TAILORED ACCOMPLISHMENTS

*If they are going to pay me over a million dollars in the next five years, I assume they'll want to know what they are getting in return.*
- Information Technology Professional

*Seeing clearly means being able to do a job interview as though you weren't the interviewer or the applicant, but someone watching dispassionately from a third chair.*
- Seth Godin, *Linchpin*

In the immediately preceding chapters, you have explored your value proposition from the perspective of your own career, taking a long-term view of what you offer in terms of skills, talents and interests, where you are career-wise and your overall target for where you wish to take your career next. This chapter now asks and helps you answer the essential question: what is the intersection between your overall value proposition and the target role for which you are actually applying in the current moment?

*Note: if your job interview is tomorrow, you may wish to scan these pages and turn directly to the workbook portion of this chapter.*

## A.    Should Your Value Proposition Be Comprehensive or Job-Specific?

You should approach your personal value proposition *both* comprehensively and specifically for the job to which you are applying. Your comprehensive value proposition is a baseline that allows you to organize yourself, dig deep into your value (in case an interviewer does the same) and think about how you wish to craft your career over the long-term. Without having done this critical "homework" to lay a foundation for yourself, it can be tempting to try to be all things to all people in a job interview and come across as a candidate who flutters from point to point – following the interviewer's lead (or perceived lead) and saying yes to everything proposed – rather than a serious and grounded professional. At the same time, if you have not become clear on your overall value proposition, you may feel that your answers sound very hollow or fake and simply recite what each employer is seeking out in a candidate (constantly changing your stripes to fit an employer's needs).

Therefore, I suggest that you first establish your comprehensive value proposition, as discussed in prior chapters, and then tailor it to each role for which you are applying, so you are ready to respond to specific needs of each individual employer. This job-specific value proposition is in many cases what is more helpful to the interviewer, who will likely not be invested in where your career can take you in the next ten or twenty years – as many candidates stay in a role for five years or less in this economy – but rather want to know what you can offer as you hit the ground running and three or six months into the new role.

## B.    Sell What Your Target Employer Is Buying

So you have explored your overall qualities and competencies in prior chapters, and the value you have and bring as a job candidate. How do you now translate this into a job-centered value proposition? By selling what they want to buy.

Let's think of the interview in a sales context. Have you ever looked for an apartment or home with a real estate agent? I have multiple times, and it can be a very frustrating experience, especially when there is more demand than supply. (Translation in the career context: more demand for jobs in your field than roles available to be filled.)

You can tell the agent that you absolutely need four good-sized bedrooms and two bathrooms, and he/she may nonetheless send listings for and/or show you homes that do not meet your needs. One may have two large bedrooms and two tiny ones. (Which kid loses out?) Another may have only 1½ bathrooms, with the agent professing: *"but it is an amazing home, you'll be lucky to get it! Look at this Jacuzzi in the master bath!"* You may admit the tub would be a great bonus – and even be tempted to consider it – but it won't help you explain to one of your kids why his bedroom is the size of a walk-in closet. Alternatively, you may say that you'll only buy a one-floor home, yet your agent may try to persuade you that "I realize this home has stairs, but they are easy to climb…." With a few agents, you almost need to threaten to or actually fire them just to have them stop wasting your time.

After reading the paragraph above, you may be nodding your head, if you have experienced this yourself. If you have never been in the market for a home, imagine another context. Buying a car, for example. If you need a car to haul things, it doesn't matter how cute the MINI Cooper Convertible looks. You won't buy it. (And if you somehow get bamboozled into buying it, you'll regret it and probably become quickly disenchanted with the purchase, unable to do what you need to get done.)

In a job interview, you are in some ways playing both the role of the agent (representing yourself) and the part of an amazing home. You have your selling features and should emphasize those, but you also need to make sure that you can and do meet the specific requirements of the target employer. The interviewer may be willing to entertain some "upgrades" or remodeling, in terms of training you to move into other areas and expand your skills, but only if you can show that your house is structurally sound, wiring is in place, everything is up to code and, most importantly, that the home (i.e., you) meets or can be easily adapted to the employer's needs. And there it is: your overall value proposition, as tailored to the requirements of the employer.

## C.    The Job-Specific Value Proposition: An Example

To understand at its core level the difference between a comprehensive value proposition and one that is job-specific in the context of a job candidate, imagine that someone (we will call her Kate) has been a musician and music producer for twenty years is now interviewing to serve as the headmaster of a private school, where she has been on the board of directors for the last five years of her music career.

What parts of Kate's current roles can be applied to the new role? Here is some background to get you going:

> *As a musician, Kate has given performances internationally and knows how to engage a crowd. She has learned how to be singularly devoted to her craft, as well as resilient and upbeat on tour and despite setbacks from time to time. Further, Kate has become well versed in the role of music and art in education and childhood development, and she has used these skills to engage children in her concerts.*

> *As a music producer, Kate has learned about business negotiations and managing the expectations of different parties to reach a common goal. She has helped other musicians create a vision for their careers, including teaching them how to make tough decisions and on occasion say "no" to certain opportunities if they are not the best fit in the long run or would pull them in too many directions. She has learned, above all, that for highly talented individuals, the problem of too many choices can be overwhelming, even if it seems like a gift to outsiders.*

> *In her board role, Kate has learned about many aspects of running a private school, from site management and finance to recruiting and alumni engagement. She has also learned how to think more strategically about the future and consider the holistic needs of an organization, while approaching problems and devising solutions with other board members, some of whom have very diverse perspectives and backgrounds.*

In the above example, I have included a number of Kate's strengths and hinted at how they transfer from one role or field to another. In the career context, these are often called "transferable skills." While I have given you a quick narrative version that illuminates Kate's value proposition and skills that would be useful in her target position, we should drill down further into what is needed for the specific headmaster role to which she is applying.

For example, the school may have a lease that will run out in three years, and it needs to search for a new location. It could have a bullying problem that has come out in recent months and is on the minds of the board members who will be interviewing her. The school may be in the middle of a significant grant application to have greater means to expand their facilities and student population, and they may need a new headmaster who not only understands (or can quickly learn) the grant-making process but also will make this grant a priority. It may have lost a beloved teacher or student to a terminal disease in the past year, and the community may feel shaken and in need of new growth and cohesion, requiring a leader with compassion and other key skills to guide the school through this time.

In other words, Kate's comprehensive value proposition serves as a backdrop and helps her interviewers understand who she is and what she offers as a candidate. On the other hand, it is not geared toward the specific needs of her new role. For Kate to be highly effective and compelling in her interview, she should be prepared not only with her talking points about her unique value-add but also about her vision and ability to address what are often called the "pain points" (i.e., problems that need solving) of her new employer (the school).

In the best-case scenario, if Kate knows that some or all of these needs are facing the individual school to which she is applying as headmaster, she can walk into the interview with a vision and value proposition tailored toward how to meet those needs. In that case, she can clearly state each issue, present her vision for how to solve it (or a range of possible solutions, if she has determined that a collaborative approach is most effective) and give examples of how she has addressed similar or analogous concerns in the past. In doing so, of course, she needs to be mindful to preserve any confidentiality concerns if she has inside information as a board member and to take the right tone, including level of details shared, for each audience.

Fortunately, since Kate is already involved as a board member with this organization, she has the perfect window into their pain points and can tailor her interview presentation to how she will meet the ongoing needs of the school while addressing these top concerns.

Not all job candidates, of course, will have the inside track that Kate does. Therefore, they will need to triangulate their efforts to uncover these needs and add what they learn to their background knowledge about what roles like their target position generally entail.

## D.   How Do You Know What Your Target Employer Needs?

Before you can determine your job-centered value proposition, you must understand what your target employer needs. There are four basic ways to know what an employer needs and, by extension, what value you can add within a specific role:

1) *Job Descriptions*. The job description for the role and for similar roles (which you can compare and contrast to the target role)

2) *Research*. The company's website and other research you undertake on the role, company and industry

3) *Informational Interviews*. Informational meetings (not job interviews) with employees at the company and others in similar roles at competitors

4) *Background Knowledge*. Your general knowledge based on experience

It is important that you consider all four categories and apply them systematically to get the best results. Most of us tend to rely on a particular source of information with which we are more comfortable and/or which is easier for us to get. This gives us an incomplete picture, of course, and at times only reinforces our long-held beliefs.

For example, some of us do extensive research while failing to undertake a critical line-by-line reading of the job description. Others rely too heavily on their own general knowledge and think they can "wing it" in an interview, failing to follow up with individuals they know on the inside of the company or in similar roles who can provide valuable information that can help make (rather than break) an interview. Still others, mainly extroverts, may talk with a number of people about the position but fail to do basic research about the company and therefore present with gaps in their knowledge about how it operates and the markets it serves.

## E. Job Descriptions

The place to start when formulating your job-centered value proposition is to read the job description line by line. After working with hundreds of clients on job search and interview preparation, I am surprised how many people, including executives, fail to do this. The job description not only recites the expectations for the job, but it often gives you insight into the culture of the employer, especially as you *compare it to other job descriptions* for similar roles.

*Not all job descriptions are created equal,* of course. Some job descriptions actually spell out what is expected in a role, while others simply recite a range of leadership, teamwork and technical skills. In a few cases, especially in bureaucratic organizations, the person who wrote the job description actually has no idea what they are looking for, so you need to dig deeper, pull from a broader range of sources on the type of role (and related job descriptions) and rely further on your instincts. At the same time, an ambiguous or opaque job description could also signal an opening for you to mold the job into a good fit, since the company may know they need help but lack the vision for what specifically will be the best use of the position. Finally, some job descriptions are vague because there is either disagreement among the principal interviewers about what they are looking for in a candidate or the company is open to adapting a role to fit the skill sets of the talent they acquire (i.e., looking for great talent and building a team around it, rather than looking to fit you, like a puzzle piece, into a pre-existing team).

Often job descriptions follow a set pattern in how they are worded, namely that they: (1) describe the company, (2) recite what the job entails (i.e., what you would actually be doing), (3) list a set of skills they expect you to have and (4) include some discussion of perks and benefits of the job.

You should pour through many related job descriptions toward the beginning of your job search, so you get a sense of what they contain, and keep copies of ones that are particularly detailed as they may yield clues that the descriptions of similar jobs have left out.

At this point, you may grasp intuitively that after reading job descriptions you can understand how they compare and contrast, but it will make even more sense to you after doing it. To illustrate with a very minor point, take a look at these lines pulled directly from online job descriptions across a range of industries and roles that describe what each company was seeking in a particular candidate. Note how often the same set of competencies or skills (discussed in the prior chapter) is expressed in a different way, sometimes with subtle differences among them.

- ❑ Ability to engage with C-level executives in a trusted advisor capacity

- ❑ Experience presenting to senior executives

- ❑ Ability to comfortably interface with all levels of management on a daily basis

- ❑ Must have entrepreneurial mindset

❑ Able to work in a changing environment

❑ Enthusiasm for working in growth stage companies

❑ Energized by a high-energy, entrepreneurial and rapidly growing culture

❑ Adaptable, able to overcome resistance to change and execute with a sense of urgency to be successful today and within the anticipated future business climate

❑ Strong financial acumen

❑ Highly developed critical thinking/analysis skills

❑ Quality driven with a passion for excellence

❑ Ability to complete projects and tasks independently with limited supervision

❑ Active mentor to junior staff

❑ Demonstrated ability to train, motivate, manage and inspire others

❑ Hard worker who is willing to work long hours

❑ Strong work ethic and collaborative attitude

❑ Ability to work well under time constraints and to meet deadlines

I urge you to begin to read job descriptions with a critical eye and make sure to read across various descriptions for related roles, so that you can understand what your target employer is looking for and tailor your value proposition to the specific job. In addition, if you find upon review that a job description hints at a work environment that would not be conducive for you, I suggest that you pass on applying to that job, rather than wasting your own (and others') time. For example, "strong work ethic" or "ability to meet deadlines" sounds very different than "hard worker who is willing to work long hours." I expect that the company who listed the latter quality they are seeking in a job candidate found that if they sugar-coated what they were looking for, this would only result in hires that became quickly disenchanted with the position. Only upon careful vetting of the company during an interview process would a candidate (hopefully) be able to discern if the employer was truly a "sweat shop" that was only interested in the *quantity* of an employee's production or one that preferred to err on the side of being honest in a job description.

In more senior roles or those with significant growth potential, of course, you need to think outside of the bounds of the job description. In interviews for senior roles, for example, you must present a vision for what you bring to the job and how both your vision and role will fit into the company's larger goals, not simply how you can successfully complete what is assigned to you. In other words, part of the value you bring is that you are focused on the organization's long-term future and have the leadership skills to help take it there.

## F.    Reading and Fitting the Job Description

As I alluded to previously, a company that describes itself as an "innovative start-up" will be very different than an "industry leader." Your presentation – from the first contact through the final interview – should communicate a value proposition that aligns with the company's view of its own brand, goals, culture, etc.

At the same time, interviewers may have specific traits or skills that they are seeking out, whether or not these are the ones generally associated with a role. A specific job description may clue you into those needed traits or skills, as it calls for a unique set of skills that is different from what you may have generated for yourself prior to knowing the specific job to which you were applying. Here's a suggestion from one early reader of this book: *Do a side-by-side analysis of the job and your competencies.*

For example, I recently reviewed a job description for an attorney position at a major financial institution in New York. If a candidate were to go into this interview and present his/her strengths in a vacuum – as some candidates tend to do, out of nervousness or lack of foresight – he/she would miss some specific skills that the employer is seeking out for the specific role. In this case, the job called for:

- Reviewing internal and market survey requests
- Supporting policy initiatives
- Evaluating risk and analyzing trends
- Preparing client reports

Armed with this information from the job description, if I were the candidate and had experience with market surveys (for example), I would be 100% sure to mention it in the early part of the interview. If I did not, I would want to make sure that at least I *know what market surveys are* and figure out if I had experience with anything analogous, so that I could "sound smart" about them.

I would further try to figure out before the interview what type of internal surveys this bank conducts and whether I could say anything intelligent about that. I may be able to get this information from someone on the inside if I had or could make a contact. Failing that, I could find out what competitors are doing so at least I could add intelligently, "No, I haven't come across that, but here's how I heard they do it at Morgan Stanley."

If I could not discern from someone on the inside either the specific institution's practices or those generally in the time I had available before the interview, I would search the heck out of it online until I came up with something, anything, so I could come across as someone who understood what they were doing and how I could help them do it. The "deer in headlights" look that arises when someone asks you at an interview if you have experience in a certain area is very often a break point, so take all costs to avoid it. If you can't avoid it, at least try to sound relaxed and intellectually curious in your response.

Gaps are unavoidable, in other words. No one can be an expert in everything, nor should that be the goal. What is important is to figure out how to bridge the gaps that do arise and sound intelligent about the process of how you will rise to the challenge. In that vein, I suggest that you take a look at every single line in the job description and ask yourself how you can exhibit the qualities, competencies and skills that can get you hired, calling in reinforcements as needed. Use a highlighter or red pen if that helps you focus on key points and outliers from prior job descriptions you have read for similar roles.

Regarding knowledge gaps, for example, an attorney with a background as an employment lawyer may wish to become General Counsel of a company and thereby become the point person for any legal issues that company may face. In addition to specific employment law knowledge, he/she must then also have a handle on mergers and acquisitions (M&A), general corporate law, corporate governance, commercial litigation, tax, real estate, executive compensation, privacy compliance and risk management, in varying order and degrees, depending on the role. The company probably will not expect the attorney to have practiced heavily in all of these areas – as few have – but will want to know that he/she knows how to identify red flags and ask the right questions when faced with an issue. What the attorney needs to do, in other words, is learn enough about each practice area to know their core concerns and be able to speak about them intelligently, while demonstrating high-level skills such as leadership, communication skills, influence, integrity, pragmatism and judgment.

## G.    Hiring Criteria

Job descriptions, of course, do not tell the full story. For example, here are the hiring criteria a data analytics executive recently shared with me for a role he is attempting to fill:

1)   Knows how to learn new things and extrapolate

2)   Sixth sense about the data and where errors may lie

3)   Ability to create insights from data, not just code or build models

4)   Ability to communicate verbally, visually and in writing

5)   Pragmatism, able to solve things and get things done

6)   True understanding of the business

7)   Sense of how to ask the right questions beforehand

8)   Resilience

Did all of these points go in the job description? No, they did not. While some of them did, the rest were in the hiring manager's head, as a set of bottom-line principles he felt would need to be met before extending an offer. After discussing his criteria, we developed questions that this interviewer could use to judge a candidate, including examples of when he/she had demonstrated the relevant qualities and skills. While all of the criteria were important, this manager said he found point 3 was often not met (the ability to create insights, not just code). At the same time, he said he felt the most important competency was point 8 (resilience), because if a candidate had resilience and seemed smart enough, he/she could likely learn everything else that was needed on the job.

This interviewer also shared that he had once asked a candidate what the code she had written was used for at her company. She responded: "It was implemented through Java." After rephrasing the question to make sure she had not misunderstood, the interviewer gave up on the candidate. As he said, "If she does not know how her work *benefits* the company and is stuck on the *process*, she will never grow into the candidate that we need her to be. She may as well be making hamburgers; she is just following orders." What he wanted to hear instead was what the model she had created was used to depict or predict, so he knew that beyond technical skills she could apply what she was doing and ask the right questions.

This same interviewer ran into a more obvious roadblock with another candidate for the same role, who either misunderstood the point of the question or was oblivious to how his efforts brought value to the company:

> *Question: Can you give me an example of some of the insights that came out of the data you analyzed?*
>
> *Answer: Well, I don't really know. I was only part of the insights team for three months.*

Another interviewer, a former information technology professional, added that at times you need to take a back door to get into a job seeker's head. She shared this advice:

> *"Want me to hire you? Show me that sparkle that is YOU. My favorite interview question for an IT interview, for example, is: 'Tell me about a piece of code that you've written recently that you loved.' Nobody asks that question. But the answers I received hands down made the decision for me personally. True geeks who loved the work they did always had quick answers for me. The answers were usually prefaced with, 'Well, it wasn't important code... really it only shaved a few minutes off of my routine work by a few minutes a week but....' The sparkle of pride in their eyes would show me a person at their best, doing what they do best. If an interviewee couldn't come up with a good answer to my question, it spoke to me about their pride in their work. It was a great question, because it had a way of giving space for geeks who didn't typically interview well to really shine. Many areas in IT have a high tolerance for poor people skills. That question allowed for some really socially un-savvy people to talk about the work they love to do."*

## H.    Research

Couple your reading of the job description with a review of the company's website and other publicly available information. Consider the company's needs as a whole and how your role will fit into the big picture. Think like the CEO or head of a business line or group, even if that is not the role you (currently) seek.

Ask yourself, if you were running the show, how would you best assemble a team of employees to meet the company's needs, and what should they collectively and individually contribute to make that happen? If you are interviewing for a role that would include a team to manage, also consider how you can demonstrate an understanding how your team fits into the company's overall strategy.

Some companies make this easier than others. Forward-thinking firms, especially those with a multinational presence who need a constant stream of high-caliber candidates, may even go to great lengths to help job seekers understand what they are seeking in their employees. McKinsey & Company, for example, states on its website that it is seeking candidates with personal impact, entrepreneurial drive, problem-solving skills and leadership abilities. McKinsey also posts tips for interviewing with the firm, which can be helpful whether or not it is your target company. See <http://www.mckinsey.com/careers/interviewing>. If your target firm does not offer this level of information, sometimes a leader in the field or competitor's site can be helpful.

## I.    Informational Interviews

Informational interviews are an important part of the research on a field, industry and company. Many job candidates – other than the truly extroverted – do not want to conduct informational interviews because they are uncomfortable reaching out beyond their inner circle and/or being in a position of needing help from others (especially if they are used to being the authority in most situations). They put off making the connections and prefer instead to rely on what they can find out by interacting with written documents – guides, blog posts, websites and the like – forgetting that their initial discomfort in the informational interview might lead to greater comfort in the actual job interview, which is where presenting well matters the most.

For more details about informational interviews, please turn back to Chapter 3.

## J.    Background Knowledge

The three data points above – job descriptions, research and informational interviews – are insightful ways to get more information about the job to which you are applying. Armed with these insights, you need to filter out what makes sense or not based on your own background knowledge.

For senior candidates (especially those who are not changing fields), this appears to come intuitively. The candidate "automatically" puts more weight on the advice of someone who sounds convincing, based on his/her view of the world coming into the conversation. Any eye-opening advice is incorporated but does not trump what is already known. Often, this judgment is hard-earned and worthwhile, but take caution that you don't become closed off to important new information or significant changes in your field.

For more junior job seekers, the challenge is always that background knowledge is scarce, and at times a candidate can suffer from information overload. As I said to a job candidate recently who found herself in this situation, the answer is not to stop seeking information from a variety of sources (although sometimes a break is needed, to avoid burning out). The solution is to stop seizing on each new piece or source of information as if it/he/she were the holy grail but instead hold close and examine disparate viewpoints, knowing there can be varying degrees of truth among multiple perspectives.

**K.      Tailored Accomplishments for each Job Interview**

On this and the following pages, you have the opportunity to tailor your skills, accomplishments and personal value proposition narrative to each individual role.

Job #1:

_____

Top skills generally required for this type of role:

_____

_____

Additional insights from job description, research or informational interviews:

_____

_____

_____

My Skills/Strengths/Edge:

_____

_____

My Gaps and how to address them:

_____

_____

Examples of how I have applied my skills that may be useful in this new role:

1) _____

_____

2) _____

_____

3) _____

_____

Job #2:

_____

Top skills generally required for this type of role:

_____

_____

Additional insights from job description, research or informational interviews:

_____

_____

_____

My Skills/Strengths/Edge:

_____

_____

My Gaps and how to address them:

_____

_____

Examples of how I have applied my skills that may be useful in this new role:

1) _____

_____

2) _____

_____

3) _____

_____

Job #3:

_____

Top skills generally required for this type of role:

_____

_____

Additional insights from job description, research or informational interviews:

_____

_____

_____

My Skills/Strengths/Edge:

_____

_____

My Gaps and how to address them:

_____

_____

Examples of how I have applied my skills that may be useful in this new role:

1) _____

_____

2) _____

_____

3) _____

_____

If you prefer a condensed format to use as a handy reference for your interview, you can complete a chart like the one below for each job interview. Additional copies are available at www.annemariesegal.com. (Click on "Worksheets.") If you don't know what to fill in below, you have more "homework" to prepare yourself and/or questions to ask at an interview!

Target Company: _____

Target Role: _____

| My Value: | Target Employer's Needs: |
|---|---|
| | |
| Accomplishments that Demonstrate My Value: | How I Meet Its Needs: |
| | |

# PART 3:

# INTERVIEW QUESTIONS

# CHAPTER 9
# THE CAPSTONE QUESTION:
# "WHY DO YOU WANT TO WORK HERE?"

*The objective drives the entire process.*
- Wendy Enelow

I initially started this workbook by writing the chapter called Interviewing 101, and then moved on to the chapters on value proposition and, only toward the end of the initial drafting, moved into this one and the last chapter (After the Interview).

In doing so, I followed the same pattern as many job candidates who spend the majority of their time going over interview tips and rehearsing ideal answers to common interview questions that may be thrown at them, only to find that they risk running out of time to prepare for some of the most important inquiries in the process: why do you want to work for the company in the first place, and why on earth the company should shell out good money to hire you?

Fortunately, I caught myself and turned my full attention here, as I hope you will as well. These questions are *front and center* in the interview process, even if they are not always asked directly (and often they are). Put succinctly, these questions are: *"Why us?"* and the related question: *"Why you?"*

As it has with everything else in our lives, the Internet has made the job search easier and harder. It is easier to find job postings than in years past, as a plethora of sites have popped up to supply us with listings. It is harder, however, to make an impactful impression on a company by simply sending along a strong resume, since there may be thousands of people applying for the same job. As a result, we send out more and more resumes, hoping that eventually we will strike gold.

Many of us then carry that same mindset to the interview process, thinking that interviews have also become anonymized, and that given the number of interviews for which we may need to prepare in order to get a single job, we should not address each company and opportunity on an individual basis but rather "conserve time" by taking shortcuts. The problem is that the approach does not work, because it turns off your interviewers. They rightly notice that you are not really interested in joining them in particular, rather just trying to get in *somewhere* and, most likely, *away from* wherever you are at the moment rather than *into* their company and the specific role. No employer wants to hire the candidate who simply papered the world with his/her resume, because that person is unlikely to want to stay for the long run, not even knowing or caring what he/she is getting into by taking the job.

So even if you feel that you cannot yet *know* why or whether you want to work at a company at the very first interview, it pays to have thought through the best answer you can give in the situation. There are a couple of key points to giving that best answer, which are captured in the subtitles that follow.

## A.      Start with the Basics

*If your **interview is tomorrow**, and you have time for nothing else, at the very least review the company's website and understand:*

(1)      the company's brand/reputation and place in the market,

(2)      what they sell and to whom,

(3)      whatever information you can learn about the specific group you would be joining,

(4)      whether you have any colleagues who already work at the employer (and, if possible, their opinions about it), and

(5)      if there are any positive customer or employee testimonials about the company or other "kudos" that you can reference.

Basically, your answer may be that you want to work for the company because (A) it is a "winner" (without saying it in so many words, but rather implying it through the details you mention) and (B) your skills can contribute to it growing even further. Of course, if the company is just coming out of bankruptcy or has had other recent troubles, the context changes, but nonetheless you want to show tempered excitement to help the company rebuild and show how you are someone to help do that.

The results of your research are touch points for your answer. If you hear good things from internal sources, mention it. If the company or group has a reputation for innovation, say that. In all cases, make sure that your answers are accompanied by how you can help the company build on its successes.

If you need a short answer to be prepared for an impending interview, you can record your initial research and responses here:

*The company's major "selling points" are:*

_____

_____

*I specifically want to work there (if known) because:*

_____

_____

*I can contribute by:*

_____

_____

_____

*I am a "fit" for the company and role because:*

_____

_____

_____

## B.    Be Excited (But Not Desperate)

First of all, be enthusiastic when you hear this question – why do you want to work here? – and (as simple as it sounds) make sure your eyes are smiling as you answer.  Desperation doesn't sell. Enthusiasm does.

As one interviewer said succinctly:

> *"Tell me why you are excited about the opportunity and our chance to work together, but don't act desperate. Desperate is never good. I will want to run as far away as possible."*

Coming across well spoken in an interview is more than half the battle. Equally important, you must demonstrate that you understand what the company does and what actually goes into a role such as the one for which you are interviewing. If you can do that – keep your eye on their needs – you will mitigate any tendency to rush into a discussion about why a job would be good for you. Again, in the context of a home purchase or apartment rental as I mentioned in the prior chapter, do you really care if the agent is in danger of missing his/her targets for the quarter? Not in the least. You are concerned about where you will live and if it meets your needs.

## C.    Remember the Central Question: Why Should We Hire You?

The question is "why do you want to work here?" The answer, however, should not really be about why *you* want to work there, but rather how you envision you can contribute to the employer. (Remember that every interview question is really the same question: why should we hire you?)

Phrasing your answer as "it would be a good opportunity for me…" or "it would be a great place to grow my career…" does not carry the day. It could be a good opportunity for the other 100 or 1000 candidates as well, and for an interviewer who has known you for 20 minutes or even a few weeks is candidly not very interested in your career; he/she is interested in what is good for the company (and meeting the needs that the role was created to fill).

Is that an old school frame of mind? In the mind of some career experts, yes. Interviewers could be more enlightened and try to sell the company (because they want to attract the best talent) rather than examine the job candidate's interview prowess, as renowned Forbes contributor Liz Ryan consistently advocates, but most of them do not. In a small number of cases, the interviewer has reason to take a special interest in you (i.e., if you are the CEO's niece, an accomplished engineer or other professional who is interviewing in a booming market, such as what now exists in Western Canada, have a unique skill or stellar reputation, or have otherwise demonstrated a special connection or talent). For everyone else, this question of "why do you want to work here?" is both a genuine attempt to make sure there is a connection and a way to screen out candidates who have not done their homework.

So get into the specifics and use the question to show that you are genuinely interested, and make sure that the reasons you give highlight your value proposition. Details about researching the company further to give more color to your answers are below.

## D.    Show You Are a "Fit"

In addition to the qualities, skills and competencies, there is also the elusive question of fit within the employer's culture that (while not everyone judges it right) cannot be emphasized enough. I am continuously surprised when job candidates pay no attention to whether there is a fit – a concept we have discussed in prior chapters – only to be disappointed time and again that they are not called back or given offers. Not only do you need to *be* a fit, but also you need to *demonstrate* a fit in the interview.

This may make the most sense with some examples. A client recently sent me a post (later filled) from the ubiquitous job search site Indeed. It was for a Senior Project Manager at a technology start-up company in Brooklyn called Zipari, that specializes in data analytics. The description of the company included keywords such as:

- Disruption [of the industry in which they operate]
- Building up [of the company]
- Complex challenges
- Teamwork and collaboration
- Motivational skills

The company then listed a number of types of individuals who make up their team, many of whom were self-described "geeks" or "creatives." From reading the job description, if you are paying attention, you can already discern that you are only a fit for this company if you can think disruptively, innovate, create and collaborate. No, I don't go far enough. You need to *love* innovation. Crave it. Live for it. And demonstrate that in the interview.

How do you demonstrate that? (If you need to ask, you may not be innovative enough for this role, but nonetheless….) When you are posed questions such as "can you tell me about yourself?" or "will you walk me through your resume?" it will not be enough to simply take a linear, serious approach. You need to present a narrative that communicates an entrepreneurial, quirky side, while showing that you enjoy complications and challenges while embracing the collaborative problem-solving opportunities presented in the role.

This is even harder to do if you are moving to a start-up role, like the one above, from a staid old institution that would not know innovation if it took a bite out of it. In that case, you have to pull from every innovative bone in your body to show how you really *are* a better fit for the new place and won't bring the same-old boring ideas with you from your current job. (Note: don't just say it. Also ask yourself if it's true.)

In another case, in a job description posted on LinkedIn, a health and wellness company in Greater Seattle called Bulletproof Digital, described its ideal candidate as having the following, among other, traits:

- You live in the PNW and think umbrellas are dorky
- You love learning, and it's one of the things you do to make yourself better every single day
- You are comfortable taking action, jumping into new projects, making recommendations, and thinking strategically
- You are a natural self-starter and don't need permission to do great things

This company has clearly given thought to the type of candidate that will best succeed in its environment. There is no need to read the tea leaves to ascertain their ideal personality type; they have put it all out there. If you need to ask what PNW means (Pacific Northwest), are afraid of "getting wet" or are more comfortable implementing others ideas than coming up with your own, this job is not the right fit for you.

Often job candidates, although they clearly can see the words on the page, read over quickly how a company describes itself without giving it enough thought. They figure that if they meet some or all of the qualifications, that should be enough, and they do not give serious consideration to "gauging a good fit" before the interview. Yet nothing is further from the truth. Quite often, there are a number of candidates with relatively similar qualifications, and the one who gets the job (even if he/she is the not the most "qualified" in an objective sense) is often the one who appears to be able to work best with the current team and the company's objectives as a whole. This gets back to why we work in the first place – to build something and serve someone, not just to earn a paycheck.

## E.    Do Your Research

Beyond what we have discussed above, tailoring your interview approach to the company, and the interviewer in particular, is a good part of what will make you successful in the interview process. So how do you do that? One obvious way is to make sure that you know as much as you can about the company.

*Note to new graduates:* if you have never before conducted research on a company, keep the notes that you make about where you find your best sources of information, so that the next time you research, it is that much easier.

If you are interviewing for a public company, for example, you should be able to uncover some or all of the points through an Internet search and review of the company's website, biographies of the senior management, SEC filings and other publicly available information:

- How do they brand themselves as a company? Is there a well-known person who is central to the brand? Is their corporate mission statement online?

- What goods or services do they offer? Are there different offerings (across multiple markets) or do they focus on one main product or service?

- If they own different brands or lines of business, do you recognize them? Do you understand (and care about) their products or services? Where can you learn more about what they offer?

- What are their revenues, net sales and/or assets under management?

- Have they stated what they expect will be (or can you make an educated guess about) their greatest drivers of growth in the short and long term?

- How many employees do they have and in what markets do they operate?

- Do they sell mainly to businesses or individuals? At what price points?

- Who are their competitors? How does the company stack up?

- How are they organized (parent company, etc.)?

- Are they highly regulated and, if so, under what laws?

- How are their board and senior management organized?

- Where are they traded (e.g., NASDAQ) and what is their stock price?

- Who are their major shareholders, if any?

- Have they had any really good (or bad) press lately? If they have had bad press, how did they handle it?

- Do they have any major projects or plans on the horizon?

- Do they have any helpful webcasts or other information online?

If you are interviewing for a CEO or other high-level role, of course, you will need in-depth knowledge of the entire company, the marketplace and its competitors, as well as vision about where you will take it next. In other roles, you will want to know more specific details that apply to the individual business segment, department or group with which you are interviewing. You may not find this information as easily online, although some facts may be available if you conduct a search with the name of the most senior person with whom you are interviewing or engage in informational interviews (discuss further below).

If it sounds like the research I suggest above is a lot of work, you are right. You cannot expect to go into an interview cold, without knowing much about the company, and impress upon them that you are highly interested in and competent for the role. While this may have worked in prior days, with the amount of information now available on most companies, you will be expected to have done your diligence before the interview.

*Do not go into an interview cold.* This cannot be stressed enough.

## F.    Prepare Your Due Diligence and Questions

List the top points you have learned about the target *company*.

1) _____

_____

2) _____

_____

3) _____

_____

4) _____

_____

5) _____

_____

6) _____

_____

List the top points you have learned about the target *team/department*.

1) _____

_____

2) _____

_____

3) _____

_____

List the top points you have learned about the target *role*.

1) _____

_____

2) _____

_____

3) _____

_____

What makes this company different and interesting from others (whether its competitors, other industries, sizes, products, etc., as relevant)?

1) _____

_____

2) _____

_____

3) _____

_____

What makes the job unique from similar roles at other companies?

1) _____

_____

2) _____

_____

3) _____

_____

Why is this job a potential fit for you?

1) _____

_____

2) _____

_____

3) _____

_____

How does this role fit into the big picture (i.e., support the company's overall goals)? If you were the CEO or head of a business unit, what would you be looking for in a candidate for this position?

1) _____

_____

2) _____

_____

3) _____

_____

4) _____

_____

What can you ask during the interview to learn more about the *company*?

1) _____

_____

2) _____

_____

3) _____

_____

What can you ask during the interview to learn more about the *team/department?*

1) _____

_____

2) _____

_____

3) _____

_____

What can you ask during the interview to learn more about the *role?*

1) _____

_____

2) _____

_____

3) _____

_____

What do you want to know about the company that you can't ask in an interview?

1) _____

_____

2) _____

_____

3) _____

_____

4) _____

_____

Where can you find this information and/or will you need to ask some of these questions in a follow-up interview or after an offer is extended?

1) _____

_____

2) _____

_____

3) _____

_____

## G.    Conduct Informational Interviews

I have discussed informational interviews elsewhere in this book, and these are great opportunities to gather more intelligence on an industry, company or specifics of a role. Especially if you are a more senior candidate, you should make an effort to set up a meeting or phone call with at least two sources to get inside information about a company. These can be with individuals on the inside, clients, fellow board members of management or the interviewer, or whomever else would have information that can help you sound like an informed candidate and help you make an informed decision. In addition, part of your response to why you want to work at the company can include the positive words given by your sources. For example: "To add to everything else I mentioned, Perry said that you all are really driven to meet the needs of clients but also have a collegial team environment...."

## H.    Prepare for Further Diligence

In addition to the questions about the company that you plan to ask to demonstrate that you understand the company and role and are an informed candidate, what else do you need answered before joining to make sure that *there is a fit on your end?* These may be questions that you save for the final interview or until after you have received an offer – because they are too delicate to ask beforehand – but they nonetheless need to be answered in order for you to make a final decision.

1) _____

_____

2) _____

_____

3) _____

_____

# CHAPTER 10
# "YOUR WEAKNESSES" AND OTHER TOUGH INTERVIEW QUESTIONS

*"If someone says they can use a software language, I need to test them on it. Otherwise, I won't know if they can actually apply it most effectively to solve the problem presented, as opposed to knowing only one way to use it. Imagine we were building a deck, and you had a guy who only knew how to nail. He would be there each day with his hammer, ready to nail, even if there was a better way to construct certain parts of the project. If I were interviewing him, my thought would be, 'that's great, when I am looking for someone to pound nails 8-10 hours a day, I'll be sure to call you.'"*
- Data Analytics Executive

Getting ready for the "tough questions" is a world of preparation unto itself, and it is where many job candidates invest the majority of their time before an interview.

If you are someone who gets "stuck" on questions and is worried you won't be able to keep up the pace in an interview without extensive preparation on the Q&A front, it makes sense to spend a lot of time running through different points you may be asked. The downside, of course, is that you could read every interview preparation book on the market, practice 500+ potential questions and still get stuck with a zinger that you never saw coming or give what an interviewer considers the wrong answer (whose opinion is, unfortunately, the only one that matters).

In the course of preparing this workbook, I have read over 30 different books on interviewing that were written by coaches, recruiters and others. At least half of the ones I found on bookstore shelves or top seller lists are written in the Q&A format, and many of these books approach responses to interview questions like learning lines of a script: "if asked X, say Y or Z, and you'll get the job."

Sophisticated candidates realize that the proposed answers may not be appropriate to an individual situation, so while they are "better than nothing," they may come across as inauthentic or off the mark. In addition, skilled interviewers will often pick up on a "canned" answer and may simply push you further until they can get you out of your comfort zone to see how you respond. The more senior you are, and the more discretion your job requires, the more you will need to go "off script" and find your own answers.

That being said, the most effective sample answers to interview questions are those that present (1) a number of alternate "winning" answers and (2) an analysis of why certain answers are better than others. The end goal, after all, is not to put on a mask and simply parrot answers but rather to understand the "call" of the question (to borrow a phrase from my law school days). Your goal, in other words, is to understand *why* a certain question is asked, so that you can give the interviewer the information hc/shc is hoping to ascertain <u>and</u> deliver an answer that resonates with both you and the interviewer.

*What is important is to know <u>why</u> a certain question is asked?*
*What is the interviewer hoping to uncover?*

For example, you may be asked, "Are you willing to work long hours?" Depending on your industry, seniority and other factors, your specific words may change, but in most cases if the question is on the table, the answer needs to be "yes, of course, I expect that is part of the job." (You can always, after the interview, decide that this is not a good fit for you.)

Sometimes, however, the right answer may be a bit more nuanced, such as, "When it is called for, certainly, although I do hope to have some control over my schedule, barring the occasional emergency." The latter answer is better delivered, of course, if a series of conditions are true: (1) you have the sense that the company already operates that way and holds the same philosophy, (2) in the context, the answer will make you sound savvy rather than uncommitted, (3) you are senior (or sought after) enough to pull it off, and (4) you are not soon facing a personal liquidity crunch that behooves you to exercise a little more conservatism in your answers.

## A.    The Weaknesses Question

*What are your weaknesses?*

When I prepare clients for interviews, this is almost invariably at the top of people's lists of questions that they are not prepared to answer. When they do have an answer, it is usually one of the "Top Three Answers" to the question or some variation thereof:

1) I am a perfectionist (i.e., my own toughest critic).
2) I work too hard (i.e., can't take a break, vacation, disconnect).
3) I am a people pleaser.

The problem with these answers is two-fold. First, that they are highly overused. Second, they don't appear to indicate any self-awareness or reflection (even if one of them is, in fact, your greatest weakness).

It is important not to underestimate this question. While many interviewers do not bother to ask it because they believe the answer will be too rehearsed, others (such as the CEO mentioned in Chapter 2) take the answer very seriously. In addition, while you should strive to find a true weakness, it is also important to put a positive spin on it and explain what you are doing to work on fixing the problem, with examples of steps you have taken to overcome them.

Here are sample answers about where your "weaknesses" may lie:

- Over the years, I have found that I don't delegate work as much as I should. I have always believed in the mantra, "If you want something done right, do it yourself."

However, I am realizing that I need to spend more time training, mentoring and building my team. In the last year, I have made this a priority. [Be ready to give examples.]

- I was never one to pay much attention to so-called "office politics" [or, I am not one for small talk] but prefer to put my head down and do my work. At some point, I realized that this would only get me so far, so I am now actively seeking out leadership [or collaborative] opportunities and focused on building relationships [across departments]. I have headed up three important projects in the last year, and I am now part of a working group that includes the CEO and other senior management.

- For a long time, I was very specialized in one area, but in the last year I realized that I needed to broaden my experience in order to grow. Lately I have taken on projects from other groups and incorporated some volunteer work into my schedule in order to cultivate a wider range of skills. I never thought – being so highly specialized would be a weakness – but I can see now that although I have become an "expert," a broader range of experiences are what I need to understand the big picture of what we are trying to achieve as a company and how I fit in.

- I have been lucky to have a very broad range of projects over my career, but I realized that I had become too much of a generalist. Sometimes you really need to get "in the weeds" on certain points, and lately I have realized the importance of having a specialty, which was frankly something I resisted. To do this, I first got certified in [X] – which was a six-month process – and I've also become involved in [name relevant organizations] and sought out projects that can deepen my knowledge in the area. [If prompted, have examples ready. Of course, this answer is only relevant if your specialty relates to the target position.]

- I have learned a tremendous amount by being the only person in my company who focuses on my area, but at times I have gone to conferences and other events and seen how much deeper my understanding would be if I had a team of people committed to the same goal. So I consider it a weakness that I haven't had this exposure. I realize that the next step in my growth is to join a team with many people working on solving the same problems, so we can mentor and bounce ideas off each other, which is one of the reasons this role is so appealing.

- I have had great success managing smaller teams of people, up to eight employees as I do currently, but I haven't yet had the opportunity to manage a larger team as I would in this role. I know that I am ready for the challenge, and I have been actively seeking out other managers who do work with larger teams to discuss the challenges of scaling up. What I have learned is….

- Early in my career, I wasn't very focused or quite sure what path I wanted to follow. I took a few different jobs, but none of them was the right match. I finally realized that what all of these roles were missing was that I didn't have a chance to connect with the ultimate customer. As soon I moved over to the sales side, everything clicked. I sometimes wish I had known from the beginning what I wanted to do, but the truth is that all of these experiences have helped me understand various aspects of the company and become a better salesperson as a result.

- My biggest weakness is that I am completely deadline-driven. I don't do as well with downtime, although I have learned to create my own deadlines to get things done. For example, I have found it very effective to break projects down into component parts, so rather than thinking of an overall deadline, I make a calendar for myself with interim dates that I need to finish certain points, so that I can keep on track.

- I consider it a weakness that I have never been very good at public speaking. Earlier in my career, it didn't matter as much, because everyone liked my work product, and so I focused on that. At some point I realized that if I was going to become a leader in my field, I needed to interact with larger groups of people across all levels. So I started to take some presentation classes and also volunteer for panels with experts in the field. I figured that the best cure to my fear was to get out and do it, and I am frankly surprised that it is working out even better than I had hoped.

- Honestly, my greatest weakness is that I still don't know my way around the corporate culture. I have had two great internships in college, but I haven't completely settled in. The good news is that I am very open to learning more and a quick study. Also, I'm fortunate to have had some really good experiences that taught me how to work across generations and build good relationships from day 1. [Be ready with examples from volunteering, travel, family life, etc. As a younger employee, by the way, being able to bridge the "Millennial-Baby Boomer Gap" is huge.]

- I would consider it a weakness that, as I am sure you have seen, most of my experience is in another industry. I have spent the last few months getting up to speed on [name of new industry] in anticipation of the change, but there is nothing that replaces actual hands-on experience in the field. Fortunately, I have two good friends who both work in [name of new industry] who have been very gracious with their time, and I also have [name any other research, connections or background that is relevant]. I know that I can hit the ground running, because…. [If you have additional time, you can discuss leadership and other transferable skills that are cross-industry.]

- It could be perceived as a weakness that for over twenty years I have worked at the same company, especially now when job changes are much more common. And it's true that I will probably never be as innovative as someone who has jumped from start-up to start-up, for example. But I have realized that I don't always need to be an "ideas man." I can hire people for that. What I have is a really strong grasp of the fundamentals, how to execute and how to grow a company. The other thing I have learned is that even the "same company" is a different company after twenty years, and having moved across different functional areas, I have certainly seen how business evolves. [Elaborate and give examples.]

These answers, as you may see, follow a certain formula: (1) identify a weakness that is specific to your professional trajectory, (2) discuss what you are doing to improve, (3) highlight something that may be obvious to your interviewer already, based on your resume, (4) are not roadblocks for you in the target role (e.g., not being a good writer in a job that requires extensive writing) and (5) characterize the "weakness" as a growing pain along the way to advancing in your career. All of these three points can be absolutely true, obviating the need to sound rehearsed, if you study your own career with some detachment.

Imagine that you were a third-party consultant evaluating your own career path to date with a SWOT (strengths, weaknesses, opportunities and threats) analysis. Everyone has each of these – S-W-O-and-T – and if you can see your own, you will be much further along in your career. At the same time, the more you consider "strengths" and "weaknesses," the more you will see that they are often two sides of the same coin. Someone who thrives on being a "people person" may not do well in a job that involves a lot of solitary thinking and problem-solving, while an introvert may not take as well to a role that requires teamwork on a daily basis and does not allow for any "alone time." These are generalizations, of course, and the goal is to figure out where you fall in this analysis, both to help your interviewer decide if you will be a fit and to help *you* sort out your best career environment, one that plays to your strengths and does not call on you to continually execute in areas of weakness.

In the context of interviewing, the beauty of a "real" answer (rather than one out of a book, even this book) to this question or others is that the true answer is not something you need to struggle to remember when you are in the interview room. If you have been actively managing your career, you will already have these insights and only need to work them into a few sentences, with examples, that you can present into the interview. If you have not been in the driver's seat in your career but instead treading water lately (which happens to the best of us), creating your "weaknesses" answer will not only be helpful for your interviews but also be a step in making a roadmap for where you would like to go next and how to get there.

## B.    The Importance of Career Check-Ups

In the same vein, if you only think about the tough career questions once a year (or every five or twenty years) when you are about to step into another interview season, then it will be harder for you to be ready to respond to them. It is a best practice, therefore, to conduct your own career retrospective or check-up on a regular basis, such as every calendar quarter, thinking about how you will improve and what examples you can give of your accomplishments.

If you have not yet had or taken the opportunity to think about your career in this way, you can start any day. Carve out the time and consider changing your paradigm from "I am preparing answers to these questions because I need to get ready for interviews" – which sounds like a chore – to "I am fortunate to be at a point that I can take a longer view of my professional career and ask myself these questions, which will invariably be helpful for my job search as well."

If you work through all of these questions for yourself – the ones above and others that you find – you will really get to know yourself as a career professional. Think of the interview less as a test and more as the opportunity to be more thoughtful about your own path.

To put this in another context that is familiar to many of us, a move from one home to another forces us to take stock, throw out what we don't need and evaluate our priorities. When moving to a new home, we decide what we want, need and can afford in terms of structure, size, possessions and lifestyle. With a fresh start, we ask ourselves how we can best create a new environment that suits our lives *at that moment* in time and *for the future*. A career change offers us that same opportunity.

## C.    Where Do You See Yourself in Five Years?

I cannot tell you the right answer to this question, but I can tell you a few of the "wrong" answers. If you have been in the job market for a while, these are obvious: don't tell you future boss you want his/her job in five years, for example.  You can't say that you are looking for a bridge job - to get you to another company or until you decide to get more schooling or retire - even if the interviewer may suspect it.

But what if one or more of these things is true? What do you say then?

Maybe you say that your five-year goal is… a greater command of [name substantive area], a chance to grow my career [list ways this role would do that] and the ability to take on [list goals or projects]. In other words, if a specific milestone is not appropriate to name, you can name what you want to have achieved in that time frame.

If you have been managing smaller projects, maybe you would like to manage larger ones. Or develop your own set of clients. Or truly master [fill in the blank]. In other words, there are a thousand ways to answer the "future goals" question, and the important thing it to make sure that your answer makes sense for the role for which you are interviewing.

As I said about weaknesses, this question is a good career check. Even if you are currently very senior and have a string of accomplishments, what's next on the horizon? Greater board interaction or membership on other corporate boards? Additional publications or branching out into writing for the first time? Taking your ideas into a new context or solving intractable or novel problems?

Most importantly, what would this new role allow you to work toward – that is meaningful to you and beneficial to the firm or organization – that you cannot achieve where you are currently? If the answers are not coming to mind, you may wish to consider whether the transition actually makes sense.

## D.    When Have You Failed at Something?

Another common interview question is:

*When have you failed at something and how did you recover?*

The point of failure should be real, tangible and relatable, but more important is the lesson, result or turnaround that comes out of it. I will give you an example from my experience:

> *A time at which I failed at something immediately comes to mind. I was working as in-house counsel, and one of our portfolio companies was being sued (which happens to just about every successful business at some point). The facts of the case were very interesting to me, and I couldn't wait to hear how our General Counsel (to whom I reported) would interpret them. He had a litigation background, which I did not, and was also adept at cutting to the chase and reducing complicated fact patterns to a set of key concerns.*

> *I saw that his door was closed but knocked anyway. When I opened the door, he asked, "Can this wait?" Instead of saying, "yes, of course" and closing the door again, I blurted out, "You won't believe what happened." After another sentence, he said, "So, it sounds like this can wait…." His eyes said everything. I should have known that this was not an emergency, and clearly whatever he was working on was more important.*

If I took this long to set up the failure in my interview response – which was one of a misunderstanding of timing and priorities – I would leave myself very little time to express what I learned from this situation. In other words, I would not be speaking as a results-oriented candidate, but rather someone who is wrapped up in the details of the circumstances. When I finally did get to the "lesson" of the situation, I might start with:

> *I went back to my desk feeling crushed, knowing I had screwed up, breaking his concentration and losing his respect. Whatever problem I had presented, with my impatience, he was probably dealing with a much larger issue.*

That might be as far as I could get given the time constraints of an interview, although if I could wrap up the problem in fewer words, I would have more time to get to the results:

> *From that day on, I always first sat at my desk first, even if I was uncomfortable with a problem. I became comfortable with discomfort and not knowing an answer right away, asking for input or guidance selectively rather than as a matter of course. I learned to extrapolate from prior situations and anticipate how the General Counsel would react, even before our conversation. Our relationship changed from that day, and I "grew up" in my career….*

It is critical that if I choose to share this failure, I get to the end of the story. It shows how I evolved from someone who needed "hand-holding" at times who preferred to abnegate taking a stand on things to one who could lead and make decisions. This is the critical aspect of the answer, not the failure itself.

When I hear the failure question, I know that there are few things the interviewer really wants to know:

> *How do you deal with failure?*

*Is failure something you learn from, beat yourself up over, see as the ultimate defeat, try to hide, run from, look around to see who or what you can blame for it or see as a normal part of learning?*

*Finally, how much resilience do you have, and will you be able to demonstrate it when needed?*

In your answer, make sure that your problem-resolution narrative about failure put you in the right light and emphasize what you learned from the experience.

## E.    Walk Me Through Your Resume

When you draft your resume you should have an eye to how it will tee you up for interviews, and when you prepare for interviews you should be pulling from your resume. These two forms of presentation (on paper and in person) do not work in isolation but should compliment each other. For example, if you highlight something on your resume that was only 10% of your workload – because, for example, it is more relevant to the position than your other accomplishments and duties – be ready to discuss it at some length. Not only should you know what you did on the project but also how it benefitted the company and what relevance it has in the larger context across companies doing the same type of work.

### COACHING MOMENT

*A client who was formerly with the District Attorney's office took a few years off from the practice of law and then reapplied for another prosecutor position. The interviewer happened to know a few judges from her old district and started asking for names of people in whose courtroom she had argued. She fumbled, having to admit that she did not remember much from those days.*

*It pays to take good notes about your prior roles and to reread them before an interview, especially if it has been some time since you have had your "head in the game."*

Some interviewers, myself included, will ask you to walk them through each role on your resume and want to know why you choose to start at a certain employer, what you accomplished and learned there and why you left. At many points throughout this book, I will discuss the importance of leaving your negativity at home and not bringing it into the interview room. When you discuss the various roles you have had, keep this in mind. The better approach is to put a positive spin on each job you have had, even if overall it was a negative experience. For example, your narrative about a role with a failed start-up may be:

*"So as you see, I left UBS to move to a start-up. I knew it was a risk, but I was young enough to take a chance, and I really believed in what they were doing. When I joined, there were only 8 employees, which soon grew to 15, and then to around 25.*

*Honestly, I think I learned more in that role in the 2 years I was there than in the 4 years at UBS. Both what to do and what not to do…. I really got to see what goes into running a company, building a management team, creating a product and taking it to market. Too bad they ran out of money. It was a bad market at the time they were trying to raise funds, and frankly they just couldn't get favorable enough terms to grow the way they would have needed. Fortunately, with what I learned from experience, I was able to move up considerably in my next role… "*

You may have been out of work for six months between the start-up and the following role – and it could have been the worst six months of your life – but by now you have intrigued me, and I am more interested in hearing how you leveraged your new skills than concerned with the gap. Don't relive those six months (at least, not in the interview). Focus on the end game: getting hired.

## F.    Tell Me About Yourself

Another common interview inquiry is to ask a job seeker: "tell me about yourself."

There is nothing like being asked to talk about oneself directly and open-endedly that can make even the most confident individual a bit nervous, and for introverts this question is often a source of great stress. While a few candidates are able to rattle this off without concern because they have a clear view of their strengths and how they fit into the role, others struggle immensely. For example, I remember spending an entire hour with a client so she could practice three or four sentences over and over, stating and refining them until the words finally flowed naturally.

I have concluded that the reason this question is difficult for many job seekers is that they do not know where to start or what to include or leave out. In other words, they have trouble putting parameters around the question. This is especially true for creative, complex individuals who have many experiences and talents to offer. Even if you have defined your value proposition and have a good sense of your brand, it is a different exercise altogether to weave these into a short presentation that does not sound like a recitation of your skills but instead comes out more naturally, as it would in a conversation.

Here's an example of a strong response to this question from a senior attorney:

> *I am a transplant from Southern California, where honestly everyone thought I was a bit too high strung. [Laughs] I moved to New York City for law school and was surprised to find that people move at the same speed as me. I fit in perfectly, and some here even call me relaxed! [Very slight pause, maintaining eye contact.] After a number of years at a top law firm, I was General Counsel of a VC fund for over 10 years, and now I am Partner at [Name of Firm] representing venture capital, private equity and other clients.*

The above is adapted from a conversation starter that I was fortunate to witness delivered over and over to clients, in various contexts, by a former colleague of mine, Gloria Skigen, Partner at Holland & Knight LLP. The clients loved her easy sense of humor, and it works equally well in an interview context. The response is self-deprecating, but in a fun and honest way, and she has opened the door for a host of follow-up questions, depending on where the client (or interviewer) would like to take the conversation next. In addition, the trait that she mentions – being less relaxed than your average Southern Californian – is not a bad quality for an attorney. To the contrary, it shows she stays on top of the issues. Note that this approach only works because the attorney in question is not "high strung" in any offensive or annoying way, she is actually very pleasant, but an extremely hard worker and consummate professional.

Job seekers who need to streamline a discussion of a transition or wish to highlight early experience, while keeping the conversation on what they can offer in the new field, can follow the same formulation as above, with a quick touch on their earlier life and then a full-on presentation of where they are today. As another law firm partner said to me recently about an interview she conducted:

> *The biggest question I wanted addressed in the interview was why the candidate had moved so many times from role to role. We thought he was a strong contender, but I just couldn't put the pieces together and needed to hear his story.*

> *We had expected to interview him in a two-person team, so while I was waiting for the other interviewer, I told him a bit about myself. When it was clear that the other person was not going to show up, I said, "So now, why don't you tell me about yourself?" I was so glad I had asked that question, because he answered it by walking me through his experience and satisfying all of my concerns about the job-hopping. It would have been a bit painful to have to ask about each individual transition, so I was glad that I could hear it altogether as he chose to tell it.*

Make sure that your personal narrative addresses the points that you believe an interviewer would most want answered. If you can do that, you are on the right track. For each candidate and *for each interview*, this may be a different answer.

In short, there are a million ways to answer the "tell-me-about-yourself" question. The best approach is to take the emphasis off yourself (and your nerves) and think about what you genuinely want to convey.

> *"I have been in health care for 20 years, starting with my first job at age 16..."*

> *"I am originally from Portland, went to school in Boston, and after a few years there have decided it is time to come home..."*

> *"People often call me a 'fixer.' Basically I come in and assess the situation, get feedback, outline a plan and help companies fix their problems. I first figured out that I had this talent when I was easily able to solve something at a prior company that had been a problem for over 20 years..."*

> *"I am one of those few people who can say with a straight face that I actually love being a lawyer..."*

> *"I studied philosophy in college, but I always had a side job doing coding of some kind or another. When I graduated, I decided that..."*

Always ask yourself: what is the story you want to tell and what do they need to hear?

## G.     Other Common Tough Questions

As you prepare for your interview, be ready for more tough questions. It is the rare interviewer who doesn't present at least a handful of these, and some even come across as if they have done a tour of Google's "tough interview questions" on the morning of your meeting.

Rather than read tough interview questions *ad infinitim*, I generally coach my clients to figure out the *type* of questions that they find most challenging. For example, you may have no problem talking about your substantive knowledge in a technical area or leadership skills, but the question of "what is your ideal job?" could send you into a tailspin. Smart interviewers will pick up on these sticking points like bloodhounds, and the questions that give you the most difficulty are usually the ones that inhabit areas of your professional life where you have the most uncertainty.

Here are some common questions that might be "tough questions" for you to answer in an interview. You may wish to star, circle or underline those that you find the hardest to answer, and then transfer the questions and answers to the space below in the workbook portion.

*What are your greatest strengths?*

*Describe a situation when you [faced an ethical dilemma, etc.]...*

*Why did you move from [X] to [Y]? [to a different field or city, for example]*

*What type of people do you find most difficult to deal with?*

*What is your preferred management style?*

*Describe your ideal job.*

*What is your leadership style?*

*What is the worst part of your current job?*

*What will you miss most if you leave your current job?*

*What gets you out of bed in the morning?*

*Do you collaborate well?*

*How do you motivate your team?*

*How do you manage stress?*

*Describe your style in dealing with difficult people.*

Tough Interview Questions    123

*What are your hobbies?*

*Are you willing to relocate?*

*Where have you taken initiative and what was the result?*

*How do you stay current in your field?*

*Tell me a time you have had a conflict at work and how you resolved it.*

*How do you deal with someone who doesn't like you?*

*Have you ever disagreed with your superiors and if so, what did you do?*

*What makes you a better hire than other candidates?*

*How have you achieved success in your current role?*

*Why do you want to work here?*

And, if it's that kind of a role…

*How many golf balls will fit in a school bus?*

This last one is a technical question of that kind that you may find in interviews with companies such as Google (and it comes from William Poundstone's *Are You Smart Enough to Work at Google?*). Please see more below regarding technical questions.

## H.    Prepare Your Answers

How do you prepare yourself for tough interview questions? Write it out or practice on your own or with a partner, but in any case make sure to run through enough questions (from the above or other sources) so you feel you are "interview ready."

Your time reflecting on your career and preparing to be witnessed from a third party's point of view is never wasted. Remember, that is all that the interviewer can offer – a point of view, whether informed or uninformed – as he/she evaluates you as a candidate.

I urge you to wrestle with the questions and, at the same time, see the "real question" being asked beyond the words expressed. (More on that below.) Ask questions of yourself (orally or in writing) or have someone pose them to you in a non-threatening environment. Find out *what your gut tells you* before you "pretty it up" for the interview.

As you are preparing your answers, don't just think in terms of yes or no, or how to provide a satisfactory response. As Robin Kessler wrote in *Competency-Based Interviews*, you need to convey to your interviewer that you are results-oriented, especially if the question is designed to gauge your competency in a certain area (of hard or soft skills).

"An astute interviewer," Robin wrote, "would expect the answers from a results-oriented candidate to be organized, logical, concise and complete. The emphasis in some of their most important answers would be on the results instead of the process." This is important to internalize and remember. Don't waste the interviewer's time on points that are not critical to assessing your candidacy. It's that same underlying query again: *why should I hire you?* Construct your answers with that question in mind.

## I.   Confrontational Questions

Most of the questions in the list above are actually standard interview fare. In a few cases, more confrontational questions (e.g., "Why *shouldn't* I hire you?) are intended to see if you can anticipate curve balls and how you react. In fact, in some interviews, the interviewer deliberately introduces stress into the conversation to see if you become rattled. You may or may not respond well to this style of interviewing – and most of us probably don't – but at least if you know it is meant as a "tactic," you can avoid taking it personally.

So what *do* you say in that case? You can treat the questions just like you would any other, taking them one by one and giving your best answers. Alternatively, if you feel that your game is off and know that if you don't address it you will throw (fail) the interview, you can address the point head-on: *"I may be totally off point, but my intuition is telling me that you are trying to see how I react to confrontation…. Or have I misunderstood the question?"* You may catch your interviewer off-guard (and sometimes in a negative way) if you say that, but you also may cause him/her to tone it down. In addition, you have demonstrated that you know how to speak directly and draw boundaries when needed.

## J.   Technical and On-the-Spot Questions

Like the golf ball question above, in some interviews involving professional candidates, you are asked to demonstrate substantive knowledge or engage in problem-solving on the spot. For example, here are some questions you could face as an operations and logistics manager candidate in an interview with Uber, the fast-growing transportation company, which appeared in an article by Biz Carson in the March 7, 2016 issue of *Business Insider*, entitled "21 Uber interview questions you don't want to be asked":

> *"Imagine you are launching Uber in a new city and have zero budget. How do you recruit drivers?"*

> *"Suppose you work at Uber. You have allotted Friday (every week) for interacting with the drivers and solving their problems. All is going on well at the start. However, on one Friday, 100s of drivers turn up together with each one having his own problem. How would you address each one of them individually?"*

> *"I am an Uber driver who claims that I did not receive my payment from Uber and thinks that Uber is cheating me. What would you say to me?"*

As if the above questions were not "hard core" enough, try this one, which the same article cites as a question for a General Manager candidate:

*"Someone was killed in an Uber and the news and social media is on fire. Draft the blog post to do some damage control."*

Tech companies and roles, as well as consulting firms, are often where you will see these questions, as well as other off-the-wall ones such as those covered by Hayley Tsukayama and Michelle Williams in *The Washington Post* on January 14, 2018, in "'Have you ever been on a boat?' and 15 other weird interview questions from tech firms":

*"How many square feet of pizza are eaten in the U.S. each year?"* (for a program analyst position at Goldman Sachs)

*"Are you more of a hunter or a gatherer?"* (for an account manager role at Dell Technologies Inc.

*"How lucky are you and why?* "(for a content manager role at Airbnb, Inc.)

One interviewer shared with me that he uses that last question often in interviews, knowing that if people do not think of themselves as lucky, they probably do not know how to create their own luck, are pretty negative in their outlook of the world or simply do not know how to engage in conversation, none of which bode well for him hiring them at his firm.

If you know that you will be facing an interview that poses this level and/or type of questioning, asks you to examine case studies or otherwise expects a demonstration of technical competence or on-the-spot thinking in the interview, this is a make-or-break aspect of your presentation. Find people who have been through the same process, applicable to your specific employer, who can lead you through how it works, the way the expect you to break down the problems and whether an exact answer or the thought-process is more important (generally the latter).

In addition, scour the publicly available information, whether it is an article similar to the one above or other sources. Finally, if you are interviewing for a larger company that has a certain set of expectations for the interview process, make sure to check whether there are any guidelines or suggestions posted on the company's website. As mentioned above in Chapter 8, see for example McKinsey & Company's interviewing tips and sample case studies on their website at <http://www.mckinsey.com/careers/interviewing>.

## K.    Industry-Specific and Role-Driven Questions

In addition to the questions above, you may be asked industry and role-specific questions, so be ready to field inquiries about your field. These can be direct or subtle, the latter in the form of (for example), "Did you see that *New York Times* article last week on…?" Make sure to keep up with the developments in your field, and also be prepared to talk shop about your industry, the company and your role in particular.

In a business development role, for example, you may be asked how you approach client relationships, how you deal with unsatisfied clients and how you think you can grow the company's business. You may also be asked if you buy their product(s) or service(s) and what your experience has been. Be ready to express an honest <u>and</u> positive response. Also, if you have them, ask intelligent questions to better understand their marketing strategy.

## L.    Why Are You Leaving (or Did You Leave) Your Current Role?

This is a "red herring" question, in the sense that it is usually asked because the interviewer is fishing for negativity, and it is your job not to convey any.

You may be in a toxic work environment. Your boss may be awful. Your company may have been raided by police or regulators. As I mention many times in this book, regardless of the reasons, negativity does not communicate well in interviews. Get your negativity out beforehand. Lock it up in a metaphorical box where it cannot touch you. You are interviewing to get away from the madness. Don't bring it with you.

Whether you are interviewing opportunistically or have been given a three-month window to find another job, you need to have a well-thought response to this question. You may have been called by a recruiter and, although you are happy in your current role, the company sounded like a great opportunity. If so, it behooves you to say that.

On the other hand, if you are on a time frame and have been asked to leave, honesty is the best policy. Make sure to state the facts unemotionally – "it is not working out in my current role because…" – and tactically move the conversation to what you have learned and, following that, can do for the new employer. Do not, instead, just say, "I was asked to leave" without giving any further details. Your interviewer will certainly have questions, and if you deal with the topic abruptly, you will raise red flags about what actually occurred that prompted the termination.

## M.    Thematic Approach to Questions

As I mentioned and have (hopefully) made clear from the structure of this workbook, it is not enough to do interview Q&A to prepare yourself for the big day. There are entire books devoted to how you can "correctly" answer interview questions, and you could spend endless days memorizing answers someone else has devised in an attempt to "beat the system" of interviewing. In some cases, that may work. In others, your answers may sound trite, especially if the interviewer has read the same books that you have or is hoping that you will open up beyond a polished, rehearsed presentation.

No matter how many questions you practice, there can always be a new one that will catch you by surprise. A better approach is to understand how *certain types of questions relate thematically with others* and prepare for how you will address each theme.

Remember, as we discussed in Chapter 2, what is the interviewer trying to do: assess whether to spend the time and money to bring you on, whether he/she can train you to do the job and what value you will add to the role and company. Hiring is risky and very expensive, and in a short amount of time, the interviewer(s) need to make an informed <u>and</u> gut decision about whether you are the one they have been looking for or someone they will wish they had dinged and forgotten.

For example, you may be asked questions that are meant to uncover your:

- *Character*

- *Personality*

- *Emotional Intelligence*

- *Work History*

- *Work and/or Management Style*

- *Ability to Problem-Solve*

- *Ability to Think on Your Feet*

- *Competence*

- *Creativity*

- *Value to the Company*

- *Readiness to Do the Job*

- *Leadership Abilities*

- *Career Goals*

- *Knowledge of What the Role Entails*

- *Seriousness About Taking the Job*

- *Credibility*

- *Trustworthiness*

If you can appreciate the interviewer's perspective and understand the reason a particular question may be asked, you will be in the best position to share information and examples that respond not only to the words of the question but the theme about your candidacy that may have prompted it.

At the same time, you can collect your mental notes based on categories of questions, such as Strengths/Weaknesses and Accomplishments/Failures. Find a system that works for you to organize your thought process and sound more polished in your answers.

**N.   "Do You Have Any Further Questions?"**

Toward the end of the interview, you will hear, "Do you have any questions for me?"

Your answer must be yes. You need to show that you have done your homework and that there is more you wish to explore. If you do nothing else I have suggested in this book, you need to ask follow-up questions.

As a medical professional put it:

> *Ask about my patients. It's why we do what we do. Be curious about the people we serve.*

The important point in the above is to show curiosity and interest not only in the role but also in the mission or goals of the organization. You will absolutely be judged by the quality of your questions, and this is one of the most important parts of the interview process.

As questions that are specific to your seniority, the audience for the question (whether a human resources professional, future boss, peer or otherwise), your industry, role and particular circumstances. For example, salespeople can be, and are sometimes expected to be, more assertive in getting to the "close" in an interview, while other candidates are expected to let the interviewer take the lead. Some different flavors of questions are:

*Is this a newly created role?*

*[If not,] what was the impetus for [or idea behind] creating this position?*

*What are the key goals for the company [department or role] over the next year?*

*What are the greatest needs to address on Day 1 of the job?*

*How is the department structured? How many people are on the team?*

*How has the team collaborated to reach a successful outcome? [good to ask if collaboration in key to the role]*

*What do you like most about working for this company [or firm]?*

*What would a successful candidate have completed 90 days into the role?*

*What would be the greatest contribution that I could make to your goals for the next six months or year?*

*Is there anything else I can tell you about my candidacy or questions I can answer for you at this time?*

*Are there any other questions I should have asked?*

*What are the next steps in the interview process?*

You can also ask follow up questions related to your company's due diligence, making sure that they are thoughtful and relevant for your role. As I mentioned in the discussion of follow-up questions in Chapter 12, you should also consider whether a certain question conveys your knowledge (and assumed knowledge given your level of seniority).

While your goal is to have insightful questions that both impress your interviewer (and answer that essential questions, "why should I hire you?") and help ascertain whether there is a fit on your end, you should not go overboard with the questions. Usually, if you are paying attention, you can judge your interviewer's availability for more questions and see that there is a natural "ending point" for the interview. When you leave the interview, if there are questions that have remained unanswered, you will generally have an additional opportunity to ask them before making a decision about whether to accept an offer.

Also take note of questions that you should <u>not</u> ask, such as those that can be answered with simple research or that put your candidacy into doubt. For example, you should not ask what you could do to improve your chance to get hired, if you do not receive an offer (which is an actual question a client of mine posed during a mock interview).

You also should not, at least in the first stage of the process, ask about benefits. The only benefits you should discuss at the first interview are the benefits you will bring to the company. This may not seem fair to some candidates – after all, you will be a valuable asset to the company, right? – but it is a highly reasonable approach to get you to your end game, which is an offer. (Note also that many of the major industry players have a "Benefits" page in the Careers section of their websites.)

What are the interview questions from this chapter or your own research that you find most challenging?

_____

_____

_____

_____

How can you prepare yourself to answer them?

_____

_____

_____

_____

For the questions you find most challenging, it can help to record your answers beforehand.

Here are some exercises to get you started.

**<u>Tough Question 1:</u>**

_____

_____

Possible Responses:

_____

_____

Personal Account to Accompany Response(s):

_____

_____

Best Response:

_____

_____

**<u>Tough Question 2:</u>**

_____

_____

Possible Responses:

_____

_____

Personal Account to Accompany Response(s):

_____

_____

Best Response:

_____

_____

**Tough Question 3:**

_____

_____

Possible Responses:

_____

_____

Personal Account to Accompany Response(s):

_____

_____

Best Response:

_____

_____

**Tough Question 4:**

_____

_____

Possible Responses:

_____

_____

Personal Account to Accompany Response(s):

_____

_____

Best Response:

_____

_____

**<u>Tough Question 5:</u>**

_____

_____

Possible Responses:

_____

_____

Personal Account to Accompany Response(s):

_____

_____

Best Response:

_____

_____

**<u>Tough Question 6:</u>**

_____

_____

Possible Responses:

_____

_____

Personal Account to Accompany Response(s):

_____

_____

Best Response:

_____

_____

# PART 4:

# UNWRITTEN RULES OF INTERVIEWING

# CHAPTER 11
# INTERVIEWING 101

With a better understanding of yourself and the value you bring to the interview table, it is time to get into the weeds and discuss what you will need to know and do in the days leading up to and on your interview day.

As in other places in this book, I suggest that you write in this section, highlighting or underlining what you want to remember and even crossing out those parts (after skimming) that you do not need to read.

## A.      Know Your Interviewers and "How You Got There"

Before you start preparing yourself for the interview, it is important to think about how you obtained it in the first place. Gary Jacobi, a finance professional and Assistant Professor at NYU, offered as a run-down of early stage questions to ask yourself:

*Did you apply for the interview or were you recruited?*

*Are you a qualified and a good fit for the role?*

*How much do you know about the company, and how much do they know about you?*

*Do you know people who work there or have other "insider" information, or do you only know what is publicly available and what you have heard about them informally?*

*Does the company only know you from your resume or are they otherwise familiar (or a relationship) with you?*

He then added:

*"Most professional interviews these days include meetings with multiple people: HR, your prospective boss and colleagues, other partners, group heads and staff, etc. When possible, know your interviewers, their titles and responsibilities and what they might be looking for in your meeting."*

Each interviewer will have his/her own agenda (i.e., goal for the interview), depending on the interviewer's role in the process. Think about what that agenda might be, and how you can help your interviewers get the confidence they need to put your candidacy forward.

Notes: _____

## B.   Don't Focus on What *You* Want

As I mentioned elsewhere, the point of an interview is not to uncover what you as the job candidate want out of a job, it is to determine whether you can serve the employer's needs. If I mention this point in a room of savvy professionals, they have learned this from experience, especially if they have interviewed others as part of their job. Any candidates who can only state that they want to work at my company because "it would be really helpful for *my* career!" or "it is the next logical step in *my* progression" have not impressed me much, and they may have even disqualified themselves from the job (depending on their other answers). Forgive the bluntness, but if I am acting as a hiring manager, I am not focused on what you want, I am focused on who can best fulfill my open position and solve the very real problems that face my company. While I may appear absorbed in what you want or what is best for your career, I am humoring you. I am not.

That doesn't mean that I won't be interested and invested in your professional development from Day 1 on the job, but until I have hired you, I am looking for what you can do for me, not the other way around.

__ I already know this

__ I need to work on this point

Notes: _____

## C.   Don't Complicate the Scheduling Process

Whether you are working with a recruiter or communicating with an employer directly (e.g., your potential future supervisor, someone in HR or an administrative assistant), take great pains to communicate clearly about when you are available for an interview.

For example, if you are asked for your availability "next Tuesday," a better response is:

*"Yes, I am available anytime after 1 pm on Tuesday, 8/16"*

(or other relevant date and time) than:

*"I am available, but not at 10 am or 12 pm, because I have meetings then."*

This answer is less communicative for three reasons, some of which may be obvious upon reading, namely that you have: (1) not confirmed that "next Tuesday" means the following week, (2) not given an end time for your pre-scheduled meetings and (3) provided too much detail about your schedule which is not relevant or helpful to anyone.

On the last point, if at all possible, you should not schedule an interview at 11 am if you have another meeting at 12 pm, even if it is intended to be only a 20-minute screening interview. If your 11 am interview gets pushed back because the interviewer's prior meeting went over (or, worse yet, if yours does), you may start at 11:20 am. That means that if you hit it off with your interviewer and go over time, at 11:45 am you will be worried that you have only fifteen minutes left until your 12 pm meeting (and have two voicemails waiting and may need to go to the bathroom) rather than focusing your full energy on the interview.

While you should strive to demonstrate as much flexibility as possible when scheduling interviews, it does not serve anyone well if you are not fully committed to the times you have made available.

Once you have an interview scheduled, you should take great pains not to reschedule, if at all possible (other than in some cases with senior candidates and those in certain types of jobs: see last paragraph to this section). Conversely, if asked to reschedule by the interviewer, you should try to do so whenever it is not entirely inconvenient, unless the new date and time would present a scheduling crunch (in the manner discussed above) or interfere with your current job or, if applicable, health concerns like necessary appointments or other high-level priorities that cannot be easily rescheduled. (There is a limit to flexibility, of course. If the employer wants to reschedule for a third time, you may politely decline to continue with the process, unless there are very convincing reasons for the request.)

*Note: if you need to reschedule an interview due to a child-related issue, such as a parent-teacher conference or babysitter who has fallen ill, I would always refer to these more generally, such as an "unavoidable last-minute meeting."*

I realize this advice may sound like a double standard, although what may not be evident is that you are one person (the job seeker) while the employer may be trying to line up multiple individuals on a single day, either to meet with you or be available to confer with the interviewer contemporaneously with the interview process. This is not always an easy task, especially around religious and secular holidays or peak vacation times.

Demonstrating the above level of flexibility may not work for every job candidate, especially ones who are working erratic and/or heavy hours to pay the bills. Nonetheless, clearly communicating and adjusting yourself to their (reasonable) expectations are the best way to avoid unnecessarily excluding yourself from interviews, If you make employers feel like they have to chase you or reconfirm in multiple communications that proposed scheduling is correct just to get you in the door, they may say, "if it is this hard to schedule an interview, what will it be like to have the candidate work here?"

*Let me drop in a caveat* for senior candidates and those who are in fields known to have unpredictable schedules: If you are an attorney who is in the middle of a closing, for example, or a CFO in the middle of busy season, it may be a better option to reschedule an interview than to appear out of sorts or distracted when you arrive.

That said, if you can keep it together during those times, you could be even more energized than usual. Remember that any rescheduling will delay what may be an already long process and can result in another candidate popping up in the meantime; however, if you are searching opportunistically, it sometimes pays to give subtle cues that (without being self-important) you have important items on your schedule that must take priority.

___ I already know how to pace myself and make time for interviews without being rushed

__ I need to work more on scheduling

Notes: _____

## D.    Map Your Route

Have more than one way to get to the offices of your target employer, in case the route you expected to take is closed. Bring a charged cell phone and/or an extra charger and leave time to navigate the parking lot if you are driving and have never been to the building before (or even if you have). If possible, check the driving, subway or bus route, walk from there and even the lobby. Not only will you see if there could be an issue, such as a lack of parking at a building's main lot or a closed street on the way there, but also you will be more familiar with the surroundings on the day of the interview, which can help make the entire process easier. As a last note, tune into the traffic and news the morning of your interview for any last minute updates.

> *I went for an interview at the courthouse in a small town. I live in a number of states away and had to fly into town for the first time the night before. I showed up at the courthouse early for the interview, and I was glad that I did. It turned out that this town has two courthouses — even though its entire population was less than 10,000 people — and I was at the wrong one. I arrived just a few minutes late to the interview, and fortunately the judge had a sense of humor about it.*
> – Law Clerk

__ I have this covered

__ I need to remember or work on this

Notes: _____

## E.    Dress the Part (In Line with Your Brand)

If you are like some of my early readers of this book, you may roll your eyes when you see advice about dressing for an interview, wondering if it *really* needs to be here (it does, of course). For everyone else who doesn't have this point down with 100% certainty, here's what you need to know:

Wear a suit, in many cases the best suit you can reasonably afford (without "overdressing" the team with whom you are interviewing), even if the office is business casual. It's an interview, not a day at the office. And while you are at it, don't forget the nails too. A clean, healthy manicure is a sign of organization and cleanliness. These are good signals to give.

There are very few cases in which a well-fitting, modern suit, in a neutral color, is not the most appropriate attire, as it shows you are a confident, serious candidate. The same goes for men and women. That said, for those cases where it is not, read more below about how to gauge what *is* appropriate. (For women, a client recently asked me whether she could wear pants to an interview. Unless there is a cultural reason not to, this is a resounding yes!)

*As I recently heard while attending a panel presentation by industry leaders who were discussing their best interview tips: Flip-flops (i.e., beach-style sandals) are the norm in Southern California, but that doesn't mean you wear them to an interview.*

In addition to the suit, which is an obvious suggestion for many readers, take note of how *every aspect of your appearance* will communicate something about yourself, positive or negative:

- The dangling earrings that bring out the color of your eyes could be distracting, so the interviewer can't focus on what you are saying.

- Your favorite shirt or dress could be too revealing or come across as evening attire. For almost every role, this is not a good look.

- Your tie or scarf may not reflect your "personal brand," or it may communicate that you have not yet learned how to wear (or tie) one properly.

- Your *choice* of suit or shirt collar may indicate that you have not had a job interview for 20 years. Trust me when I say that is not a good look.

- For both men and women, your choice of hairstyle is your own, but your hair still needs to look professional. I have had a number of interviewers comment that a candidate's hair was distracting. In one case, the interviewer said, "His hair was literally sticking straight up. I mean, what kind of a look is that?" This particular comment was, by the way, in the context of an interview at a healthcare firm (not for a role as a performer in the music industry or another environment that might have a special view of personal style).

**In general, assess what type of an environment are you walking into, and how can you look like you belong there. Fit is one of the most important points that an interviewer is trying to assess.** That said, know your environment, to the extent you can assess that before the interview. If you live somewhere that it's just too hot for a tie or pantyhose, and no one ever does it, don't show up looking stuffy. **Know the right fit.**

*CAVEAT:*
*If You Know the CEO, Dress to His (or Her) Taste*

A hedge fund trader and executive (who has had other roles, including on the inside of a major company) had the following caveat to the general rule about wearing suits, in this case relating to knowledge you may have from prior dealings with a Chief Executive Officer:

*"If you know the CEO personally, you may know that he likes to wear shorts and a T-shirt to work every day in the summer and views with suspicion people who wear suits to try to impress him.*

*In that case, you will make him more comfortable if you dress like him and show that you understand what he prefers. A nice polo shirt, khaki shorts and sandals work better than a suit for this particular type of interview."*

I think this advice is right on, especially if the CEO wants to know that everyone on his team can play to his tune and get along with the other players. In other words, it is important to know the tone set at the top.

That said, this move only works if you actually do know the CEO, you are sure any other interviewers you have will appreciate the gesture and you are senior enough to pull it off. You are taking a risk that could backfire, but sometimes playing it safe doesn't get you anywhere, especially in an environment that rewards calculated risks.

The above advice – to skip the suit – can apply to other situations in which an entire office "dresses down" or is creative/artistic in dress and expects its interviewees to match its message. In that case, you are still branding yourself to fit into the environment, and if it is a better match for your own personal brand, that's a win-win. If in doubt, ask a trusted source or make a decision based on your risk tolerance (for being wrong) and comfort level with either choice. If you are highly confident in your abilities, you can let your calling card be your talent, not your tie. Alternatively, you can meet halfway, wearing a suit but showing your originality or points of difference through your choice of designer, color, style or fabric. The less conservatively you dress, the less choices of employers you may have, but the ones that do want to hire you may be a better environment for you overall.

For example, I once interviewed and hired a young woman (who later earned her MFA from Yale and has become a celebrated artist) for an entry-level arts administration position at a major bank. She did wear a suit to the interview, but it was chic vintage and completely out of character for "bankers," as were her funky glasses. I assume she did not think of this as a *personal brand* in the way that we have defined it in more recent years, although that is exactly what it was. Her style said, "OK, I'll wear a suit, but *my* way." Her attitude conveyed the same thing: "I'll be a great employee, but I won't pretend to be something I am not." I loved her immediately, and she was my best hire, miles ahead of her boring navy-blue-suit colleague whom the department had also just hired and needed to fire a few months later (he was clearly clocking in his time, made countless errors and had no passion for what we were trying to accomplish). In fact, this same artist I had hired continued to move up at the bank after I left, staying on for six years.

### In My Experience: Every Detail Counts

*I once interviewed a junior candidate who had scrapes and huge red scabs on both knees. For at least a portion of the interview, rather than focusing on her answers, I found myself distracted wondering why she didn't wear pants (rather than a skirt) or at least dark tights to cover it up. I wondered if she lacked attention to detail and would exercise good judgment in other matters.*

*There could be many reasons why this candidate did not have an appropriate outfit that would cover her scrapes. She may have lost or gained weight recently (yes, really) and didn't have another suit that fit. She may have left all of her interview attire at her parent's house, not expecting an interview yet, and was forced to find something to wear at the last minute. It could be that the scrapes had happened the morning of the interview.*

*The truth is that, as an interviewer, I did not care what the reason was (small caveat: if she had told me it happened on that morning, it may have changed my mind, if I believed her and she did not spend time elaborating but simply moved on to the interview after that). My job was to choose the best person for the firm, not imagine with excuses for a candidate's lack of professionalism.*

*This may sound harsh – and I admit I am a tough interviewer – but as they say, business is business. You only get one chance to make a good first impression, and I can only make decisions based on the "package" presented.*

### *A Registered Nurse's Perspective*

*An experienced nurse at a top multi-specialty and research hospital had this to say about the choice of wearing a suit vs. not wearing a suit:*

*"I expect an experienced RN to have professional dress. I cut slack to new graduates who may not have the resources for professional scrubs, but I note that professional scrubs are NOT 'blues' or 'greens,' which is what many in healthcare wear day-to-day. Operating room (OR) scrubs are <u>not</u> appropriate for an interview."*

**In summary, your choice of clothing for the interview should match the environment, but it should also reflect your personal brand (which include your philosophical, cultural and religious choices).** With the above in mind, my usual advice to job candidates is consistent: dress as you would for an important client meeting. That way, you will feel at your most confident, and the interviewer can imagine sending you out as a member of his/her team and representative of the firm.

Final note: if you have an inkling that you need a professional stylist or image consultant (or at least the advice of a trusted sibling, cousin or friend) to enhance your appearance or clarify your clothing-as-personal-brand, then by all means, enlist the help!

___ I can't believe you think I need this [**note:** read the caveats below]

___ Thanks for driving this point home

Notes: _____

### F.    Bring Backup

If you have never had your pantyhose run while hopping out of the car, gotten a bloody nose all over your new shirt, had a button on your pants pop off unexpectedly or otherwise had a last minute malfunction in your wardrobe, heed the advice of those who have. You will be glad to have extras if and when you actually need them, and the preparation time is minimal.

As far as your resume, I would bring three to five extra copies, depending on your seniority and stage in the process. Even if the interviewer has printed out a faxed or emailed copy of your career documents, seeing a fresh version on resume paper is bound to make an impression with just about any interviewer (including those who may be invited to meet with you last minute and may not have had a chance to study it closely).

The job description is also helpful to bring because, believe it or not, there are some interviewers who may not know or remember everything written there. You may say, for example, that you were excited to see that the position called for a unique skill that you happen to have and find that your comment is met with a blank stare at the other side of the table. If you have a copy of the job description, you can say, "At least I think so… hold on, yes, here it is…" then politely pass the specifications to the interviewer and what would otherwise have been a he-said, she-said moment is now simply a matter of reading what is printed on the page. Your interviewer may still wave you off by saying that the job description is incorrect, but your credibility for knowing what you read is intact.

The reason for the phone charger is to make sure you can access GPS (if available) in case your usual route is blocked and you are running out of battery. This can happen even on routes that are well known to you, because a tree is down, the subway is running late or a multi-car accident has halted traffic. If you do not have GPS as an option due to technology or location, I would print out three routes from Google Maps or another service, so you have a backup plan. If you never need them, they are like the proverbial backup plan: bring an umbrella so it does not rain.

___ I always bring an interview "emergency kit," including a cell phone charger, extra copies of my resume and the job description

___ I need to put this together and/or remember to do this

Notes: _____

## G.   Play Nice in the Parking Lot

**The interview starts the moment you make your first contact with the company, whether it is at the reception desk or beforehand (including online interactions).  It can start even sooner if you know the company from prior dealings with them, e.g., if they are/were your client or you are/were theirs.** If you did not observe this practice before reading it here on the page and following the advice affects the outcome of your interview, you may have just recovered many multiples of the cost of this book.

*Hidden Interview Moments*

Start now by treating every possible interaction with anyone connected with the company – from its secretaries to its suppliers – like a screening interview for your next job. While you list your formal references and expect that they may be called, savvy interviewers know that they get their best information from the people you did not put on the list.

In this same vein, every correspondence, phone call and meeting that you have with the company is an "interview" in some sense. Take care with writing proper emails (from a professional email address, e.g., firstnamelastname@gmail.com), check LinkedIn messages regularly (tip: have notifications sent to your email) and respond with the same care and treat an informal call from a company recruiter or HR person as an impromptu interview (and know that it may blossom into one, so only answer when you are in a place that you can properly address the call).

*First Impressions*

I am sure I do not need to tell you that first impressions matter, but unfortunately not everyone heeds this advice. In some cases, you may not realize that you are even making a bad first impression, so it pays to be always vigilant.

> *You may have heard the story of the young woman who was in a big hurry to get to an interview. Running late, she cut off another car, whose driver honked at her in response. She frowned, held up her middle finger and drove off. And, wouldn't you know it, the person she flipped off in traffic was her interviewer that morning. She did not get the job.*

Few of us will face this particular scenario, but more of us <u>will</u> forget that everywhere we go within the proximity of the target company, we may see someone who has control over or input into the outcome of the interview process. This means you need to be respectful, polite, outgoing and forgiving in, for example:

- The parking lot

- Men's or women's rooms

- Elevators

- Reception areas and lobbies

There are quite a number of interviewers who have figured out that if you treat people poorly when they are not looking during the interview, you will continue to do so as an employee of the company, which can kill morale. Some environments still allow this type of behavior, of course, but it is becoming more common to expect all employees (even the top producers) to exhibit a modicum of civility.

At the same time, make sure that your first impression upon meeting your interviewer is also a good one. You don't want to be so buried in your phone that you do not hear your name called, for example, or slumped over in your chair when they walk in the door. If the room in which you are waiting has a view, it is perfectly acceptable to look out at and admire the view. You do not need to wait in your chair looking like a stuffed shirt. This gives you the ability to be standing when your interviewer enters, look him or her in the eye, have a conversation starter and show some admiration for the company (via the space it inhabits.)

___ I already do this

__ I need to work on this

Notes: _____

## H.    Find Out and Remember Everyone's Name

Every single person with whom you meet at the company can be asked back to report to the interviewer and ultimate decision-makers about your behavior and demeanor during your visit. While you do not need to remember that the receptionist's name is Kristina and that she is originally from Madrid, you can bet that if you do you will make a better impression on her than someone who barely notices her on the way through the door. In addition, you should take pains to get emails and correct spelling of names for anyone who interviews you, so that you can send proper thank-you notes. The easiest way to do this is to ask for a card, and if someone does not have one, you can check with your new friend Kristina to get his/her details. (See Chapter 16 for more on the topic of thank-you notes.)

__ I already do this

__ I need to work on this

Notes: _____

## I.    Keep Your Family's Finances to Yourself

This advice is generally directed to the younger graduates, especially those for whom no topic was off limits at home. Don't talk about how much wealth your family has or does not have, and while you are at it, leave out other hot button topics such as politics and personal religious beliefs, unless the job for which you are interviewing is about those very topics. Whether your family has a personal island where you vacation on extended weekends or you have cousins have joined a cult, keep it to yourself.

I will never forget the interview lunch I had with a partner of my prior law firm and a summer associate (who was essentially on "probation" until receiving a virtually guaranteed offer of full-time employment). The partner lamented at one point about having to work so hard, and the summer associate later leaned over to me and whispered, "If he would sell his house upstate and tell his wife to stop shopping all day, maybe he could take a break."

While I didn't recount the summer intern's words to the partner – I was still young myself, and I felt it was too embarrassing to even mention – I was later told that this individual would be the only one of the summer class who did not receive a full-time offer. His work quality was fine, but he had made similar comments that got back to senior management. In short, they were concerned that he would alienate our clients, not to mention offend his superiors (over whom he saw himself as "superior," hence the problem).

As an interviewer, I don't need to know your financial information, whether good or bad. Don't tell me that you have just taken out a loan for a new house, had a lot of medical bills last year or anything else about your finances. That information will probably deter me from offering you a job, especially if I am concerned that you will be cash strapped and looking for a raise six months into the job (whether or not you have earned it).

__ I have this point under control

__ I need to work on this

Notes: _____

## J.      Be "On" for Interview Day

Treat your interview as if it is the most important task in your day or week. It probably is. Eat food that gives you energy, wear clothes that you can move and breathe in, listen to music that you love and crank the A/C if it is a hot day (or take alternate transportation if you would normally ride the subway).

Do whatever it takes to be "on" for the interview.

__ I know what I need to be rested, prepped and psyched for interviews

__ I need to find my interview-prep groove

Notes: _____

## K.      Know What is On Your Resume

One of the worst things that you can do in an interview is scratch your head, go blank or struggle to get the words out when asked about a prior role on your resume. If you wrote on your resume that you "conducted 25 [so-and-so's]," you had better remember what a so-and-so is, why it mattered, what your goals were in doing it and how it benefitted the company.

If you cannot remember what you did in a job from years past, find a way to refresh your memory, whether it means calling up old colleagues or doing some research to find a similar situation and piece it together.

*On the other hand, do not expect that your interviewer is 100% familiar with your resume.*

He/she may have read it three weeks ago and decided you went into the "we should interview" pile but not had a chance to look at it since. One of the worst comments to make to an interviewer is to say, "Of course, if you had read my resume, you would know that." While most of us know that, we can unwittingly communicate the same expectation through tone or body language. Be excited to share your resume with the interviewer, or it may be your last chance to do so.

Another tip about resumes: when I say have it in front of you, I mean to *literally* carry it with you to the interview in a professional briefcase, set it out on the table neatly and treat it like an important document.

Don't, for example, pull it out of your bra. While it sounds like a joke – and a levity break is never a bad idea – this advice comes straight from my direct conversations with interviewers. It's another comment from the nurse I quoted above:

> *I actually had a nurse come to an interview and pull her resume, neatly folded, out of her bra. You would think that you wouldn't need to tell people not to do this. In nursing, it seems to be more of an issue with new grads who have not learned how to prepare themselves properly. I wish I could tell you that the bra story wasn't something we still laugh about, but I suppose we are small and petty, and we do. ("Did she pull her resume out of her bra?" is a valid question in my clinic, accompanied by snickers.)*

__ I will have five copies of my resume neat and ready, on resume paper (in the version already provided to the employer, or an update if my circumstances have changed)

__ I need to prepare this and have it ready

Notes: _____

## L.    Say "Yes" to Water or Coffee

When you arrive at your interview, you will likely be asked if you want water, coffee or something else to drink. Say yes, even if you don't plan to drink it.

Being polite, getting along, building a connection, extending the conversation and obviating a need or desire to ask for something later in the process (after declining) are all positives in the interview process. Take advantage of the opportunity to build the connection. In addition, the room in which you will be interviewing may be hotter or drier than expected, and the interview may go on longer than expected, so you may be very glad you have something to quench your thirst or keep you focused. One interviewer even mentioned to me that he has had three candidates sweat so profusely in interviews – due to nerves, not the heat – that he has left the room to bring them the water they had earlier declined. None of them, incidentally, were hired.

As in some other cases in this book, I should throw out a small caveat here. If your interviewer looks extremely rushed and offers water or coffee as an afterthought but appears to want to "just get down to business," you can pass unless you think you'll actually need it. I often bring a water bottle tucked into my bag as a backup for that very purpose.

## M.    Be Aware of Your Eye Contact and Body Language

On eye contact –

I have been obliged to make this comment so many times in interview preparation sessions with clients – and have seen the problem live as an interviewer – that I am betting more people fail to make proper eye contact than you would suspect.

The goal is not to make *constant* eye contact, but rather to make sure that you are doing so at critical times, such as when asked a question about accomplishments or challenges. If you look away when asked a direct question, whether in person or on Skype (where it is even more obvious, since ambient details subside and the interviewer is fully focused on your face), it can appear that you are avoiding the question, even if you are simply casting your glance wide to recollect a situation or gather your thoughts.

On body language –

There are entire books about how to use body language to your advantage, and we certainly cannot cover all of it here. In addition to proper posture – and not leaning too far forward or back, not sitting too hunched or too rigid – watch whether you use your hands too much and if you generally carry yourself as a confident person. If you have not given thought to body language recently, I suggest that you learn or brush up on these skills.

I have often suggested to clients that they practice interviewing by taking videos of themselves, which is easy enough to do with any modern phone and a "selfie" setting for the video. You can set this up in a quiet room or, if you have no private space, even try it in a car (parked, of course). Hear and watch yourself answer. Note what you say, how you say it, where your eyes go, whether you sound friendly, etc. While you will not get the full effect of a true "mock interview," you will have new insights that can help you be aware of how you present yourself. Don't worry; no one needs to see the videos later.

On another point, make sure to have a firm handshake that is neither holding back nor crushing the interviewer's fingers. This crucial first impression can make an important difference in someone's view of you as a candidate. If you have any doubt about your handshake, ask for honest feedback from a few honest sources.

\_\_ I already do this

\_\_ This part of my presentation could use work

Notes: _____

## N.    Notice Non-Verbal Cues

In interviews as in other important interactions, it is critical that you make sure to hold the attention of the person in front of you. When asked to discuss your resume, for example, if you find that you are going off on a topic that is "losing" your interviewer or he/she no longer responds with enthusiasm, you will need to adjust your tone, speed or topics of conversation.

If you are not good at reading cues, first follow the interviewer's eyes. Is he/she still making regular eye contact or instead staring down at your resume, looking out the window or, worse yet, checking his/her watch? Also, does your interviewer look engaged or have a pained expression? Having conducted many interviews myself, I am consistently amazed when job seekers seem to talk into a vacuum, carefully reciting their prepared speeches while almost seeming to forget that I am in the room.

\_\_ I already do this

___ I need to work on this

Notes: _____

## O.    Speak Confidently

For those job seekers who are and come across confident in interviews, kudos to you. (If you are *not* confident but freaking out instead, see the advice in Chapter 13.)

For those who are unsure about how to communicate their accomplishments or otherwise fail to present with authority, these are major points to improve. Although you certainly may still get "a job," you will not get the role and compensation you would otherwise be able to obtain if you cannot present yourself as a compelling and convincing candidate. Take public speaking classes, join an improv group, work with a coach or conduct mock interviews through your university career center.

Do what it takes to be more comfortable opening up and letting the world know what you have to offer. If you need to spend money to get yourself there, generally your higher compensation will offset whatever expenditures you make.

As an ancillary point, pay attention to your voice and whether it sounds warm *and* powerful at the same time. Keep it steady. Don't let your tone move into the form of a question as you answer something you are hesitant about. While you should admit what you do not know, try to sound confident at all times.

___ I already do this

___ I need to work on this  (___ a little bit or ___ I need major help)

Notes: _____

## P.    Be Ready with References and Supporting Documents

You should be ready for background checks and have three or more professional references (who know you well) available to speak with the interviewer when requested. Often, these should be former direct and/or indirect supervisors, although sometimes other references are appropriate, especially if you are a new graduate or will be changing fields.

Provide your references with an updated copy of your resume and some information about the type of roles that you are targeting. In addition, refresh their memory about the work that you did under their supervision or on other points that are applicable to your candidacy.

As Brian Bodkin, President of Career and Talent Hub, shared:

> *"Call up your references and remind them of how you worked six days or sixty hours a week on the project they supervised. Give them any information they need to recollect how you excelled as an employee so that they can make a strong, positive recommendation."*

This is true even if you have maintained contact with references since leaving a prior job. Put the information at their fingertips!

If your field or role requires it, you may also need to have other documents ready, such as a writing sample (e.g., for law firm jobs). It is a good idea to start preparing these documents long before they will be requested.

__ I already have these available

__ I need to prepare these

Notes: _____

Of these fundamental interview points, my greatest challenges are:

_____

_____

_____

My plans to address these challenges are:

_____

_____

_____

Points I want to remember for the interview day are:

_____

_____

_____

# CHAPTER 12
# BEYOND 101:
# REFINING YOUR INTERVIEWING STYLE

The points in the prior chapter (Interviewing 101) are what I might call "basic interviewing skills," although not everyone who has been interviewed multiple times can profess to have mastered them. The points below speak further to how to refine your interviewing style and create the best "interview package" for the job or, in some cases, are more specific and sophisticated ways to approach the interview process.

## A.      Communicate Your Value

*Note: I covered this point separately under the "value proposition" section, but it is important to mention here in case you have flipped to this chapter directly. If you have trouble speaking to your value, I suggest you review the Value Proposition section of this book.*

Know the 3-5 points (depending on the length of the interview and the seniority of the role) that you want to drive home in an interview – why you are the best candidate for the job and how you can benefit the company – and make sure you find a way to weave them seamlessly into your interview responses. You are not looking to write a script for yourself, but instead create a direction for your interview responses and narrative about your candidacy.

### Coaching Moment

*I was helping a client prepare for her interviews, and she has a background that has taken many twists and turns. She has gained many different skills as a result, but she is concerned that someone may find her path disjointed or exhibiting a lack of focus. (Honestly, for some period of time at least, it was.) We discussed how she could sum up her seven different roles in the last 10 years with two or three main "work themes" and present them as a positive package – the diversity of experience and her resulting big-picture perspective is indeed a good part of what she has to offer – rather than feel inadequate against a sea of so-called stronger candidates.*

\_\_ I know how to message my value

\_\_ I need to work on this

Notes: _____

## B.      Speak to Your Future, Not Your Past

Regardless of the specific question asked, you need to *sound* like the role that you are seeking to fill rather than the one you are leaving. For example, if you are changing careers, learn the vocabulary of your new field or industry. If you are leaving government, the military or academia for the corporate world, for example, learn how your future colleagues see the world, which can be vastly different from what you have encountered in the past. If you are straddling two fields, industries, etc., sound more like your new one than your old. For example, if you are moving from a traditional role at a big firm (i.e., strong and steady) to a small one (i.e., nimble and entrepreneurial), be sensitive to the differences. Don't sound like you only "fit" where you are leaving, but instead speak to where you are going.

There are many ways to become more familiar with a new arena, including books, articles, informational interviews, seminars, other trainings and even YouTube videos put out by your target companies and their competitors.

___ I already do this

___ I need to work on this

Notes: _____

## C.    Adapt Your Strategy, If Needed

If you go into an interview with your entire preparation geared toward a certain style or set of questions that you anticipated would be presented, and the structure or strategy of the interview turns out to be completely different, you need to be ready to roll with it. Think about it this way: there is no turning back the clock and preparing again, so you can either get with the program or come across as someone who can't.

___ I am ready to do this

___ I need to remind myself of this on the morning of the interview

Notes: _____

## D.    If You Get Stuck, Get Yourself Out of It

No matter how much or well you prepare for an interview, you may that you get "stuck" (without words) in the middle of the meeting. For example, you may lose a train of thought or simply not know how to answer a question. Or you may say something that you realize, as it is coming out of your mouth, that you should not have said.

Be kind to yourself in that case. It happens. Don't stay stuck; get yourself out of it.

How do you get yourself unstuck? One way is to simply create more time to respond. For example, "That's a good question… Let me think about that for a moment…." The few seconds may be enough to get your thought process in place.

If you are considering two examples and wondering which one is the best to present, use your "why should we hire you?" antennae to help you decide. If you are interviewing for a marketing position, use an example that shows off your marketing skills. If technical, talk about when you solved a technical problem. If you know the company is suffering from a lack of leadership, and this is what they are looking for in a candidate, make sure your examples reflect your leadership skills.

### Coaching Moment

*I was working with a student to prepare him for an interview. He mentioned a situation where he had gotten stuck in the past, and he was worried that he might again.*

*After telling a potential employer the three main reasons why he was interested in a certain job, the interviewer asked why else he wanted the role. He was stumped. He could not think of any other reason to give.*

*My client then told me that he sat for what felt like five minutes — but may have only been one — in silence while the interviewer stared at him, waiting for an answer. The more time passed, the more nervous he got. Finally, he said that he didn't know. For the rest of the interview, he gave minimal answers, just waiting for the chance to leave and stick his head under the covers.*

*While I was not in the room during the interview (of course) and cannot attest to the overall mood and line of questions, the advice I gave him to do differently in the future is as follows. If you don't know what to say, you can at least walk the interviewer through past responses as you think of what you'll say next. "Well, as I mentioned, I would like to work here because [reasons 1, 2 and 3]... And also because...." At that point, if you have nothing more to add, you can flesh out more of one of the reasons you have already given. Think of the interview like a tennis volley. Sometimes, if you can't take your best swing, the second best response is to get the ball to the other side of the net.*

___ I already know how to do this

___ I need to better prepare myself for this

Notes: _____

## E.    Have Follow-Up Questions (Yes, Really!)

As I mentioned earlier, if you are asked if you have any follow-up questions, the answer should always be yes. This is your grand opportunity to demonstrate your thought process, research on or knowledge about company, general industry/area knowledge, curiosity, enthusiasm and judgment in appropriate questions to ask. Good follow-up questions are appropriate to the firm or organization, your seniority and the role. Some examples are listed in the last section of Chapter 10, and others may arise in your own research.

Generally, your follow-up questions should not be focused on work-life balance, salary, benefits, workload and hours expectations, and the like. These points are usually best discussed and/or negotiated after a hard or soft offer is in hand (or at least until you are further along in the process), unless one or more is a deal-breaker on your end. As I explained to a client once, your goal as a job seeker is (with slight exaggeration) to be paid as much as possible and still get the job, and their goal as an employer is to pay you as little as possible and still have you as an employee, but neither of you should admit that. First prove you are the best candidate that they <u>need</u> to hire, and you will be in a better bargaining position when compensation points do arise in your negotiations.

### *In My Experience: What You Should Know Before the Interview*

*While interviewing people for a role at a hedge and private equity fund, I had a candidate say that she had done some initial research on the difference between "hedge funds" and "private equity funds" and understood some initial points but was wondering if I could flesh out the differences. She then gave me three examples of differences she had already uncovered. This was for a paralegal role, so the question was entirely appropriate and indicated she did her homework but was willing to admit that there are things she doesn't know rather than pretending to know everything (an important quality in many fields, especially ones that require highly accurate work product).*

*On the other hand, this question would not be well received if the candidate were applying for a front-office position or a general counsel, CTO, CFO or other high-level role. In that case, more specialized knowledge about the industry and specifics of the firm is assumed, and the candidate's questions should come out at a much higher level, related to the big picture of the business or the specifics of the department or role.*

\_\_ I have follow-up questions ready

\_\_ I need to work on this

Notes: _____

### F.    Trust Your Gut

If you have read this far into the workbook or simply flipped to this page, it is helpful to insert a quick note that there are very few "hard and fast" rules on interviewing that must be followed in all cases despite the name of this portion of the workbook. Therefore, take any advice that you read here or gain from any other resource – including advice from mentors, friends, books and sources on the Internet – with the proverbial grain of salt. None of us are with you in the interview room, so none of us should be making the final call on what will work or not work with a particular interviewer.

Nevertheless, when you trust your gut versus the so-called best advice, do not forget to actually *follow your gut* (i.e., that smart voice in your solar plexus, not the nagging one in your brain). By this I mean, for example, if you have received consistent feedback that you share too much personal information in interviews, you should not assume that in a particular case you are "justified" in sharing that information, because the interviewer seems interested.

*Whether or not you are justified to say something in an interview or your stress will be relieved by doing so* is not the most important thing.

*The most important thing is* to get an offer (while staying true to yourself and your values).

Imagine I told you that the way to ace an interview is to have yogurt that morning. (I wouldn't, but for sake of argument.) If you know you hate yogurt or are allergic to dairy, you may assume my advice was generally sound but still decline to follow it. The same goes for interviewing. Follow good advice, but not blindly.

Always take the big picture view, as if you were viewing yourself from a vantage point above or watching your performance from the room next door. What will best position you to advance your interview goals and be authentic to yourself? Do that.

__ I have rehearsed and am ready to give "the right answers"

__ I know how to trust my gut

Notes: _____

## G.    Leave the Negativity at Home

As I mentioned above, leave the negativity at home.

If you are exhausted from your current role, upset that you haven't found a job yet, annoyed or hurt that you were let go from a prior role and/or confused about professional or personal decisions ahead, get all of this out somewhere else (in a safe place), and don't bring it to the interview.

> ### In My Experience: "Off the Cuff" Remarks Sound Unprofessional
>
> *In my prior role as a law firm partner, I was once interviewing a New York City attorney for an associate role in the Connecticut suburbs. It was a screening interview, suggested by a referral. At one point, I asked the candidate if she was interested in working in Connecticut and would be open to getting Connecticut bar admission. She let out a long sigh, paused and said, "Well, I have been wondering about that myself. I guess it is worth it if I get the job, since I haven't been able to find anything in New York. It is honestly really hard to find anything, so I am kind of open. We have also considered moving to New Jersey…. So to answer your question, if it's required to work at the firm, I guess would get admitted in Connecticut… I guess."*
>
> *While she had made a number of other interview faux pas along the way, some of which I may have overlooked given the strength of the reference, it clicked for me at that exact moment that she was not the right person for the job. We wanted someone who was excited about working with us and committed to staying for the long haul (or at least five years). Her answer communicated that she was neither. Instead, she was noncommittal and even dismissive in her responses.*

If you have a tendency to self-sabotage, work this out before you get into the interview room. In the example above, the interviewee was wondering herself if she wanted to take on the requirements of the job. This was something she should have answered for herself beforehand, so she could deliver a response with conviction. At the end of the day, it is a "yes" or "no" question – and it deserves a simple answer. Frankly, if you are not enthusiastic enough about a job to bridge a gap between your current competencies or certifications and what you will need in the role, then don't accept the interview.

If you have bad news to deliver (or rather, to confirm if asked) in an interview, such as the fact that you were fired from a job, the best thing is to explain it in a few short sentences, in neutral terms, and move on. For example, "and what I learned from this is…."

Sometimes it is very hard to create a narrative around why you are leaving, especially if the reason is that the place is falling into shambles, since you can't quite say that. With a very senior client in that situation, we recently decided that the most honest, yet guarded, answer she could give was: "The company has changed since I joined, and some of my closest colleagues have left, so it seems like the right time…" Any answer needs to be sincere – and not overdone or apologetic – so think carefully about a clean, accurate and professional way to express it. Also, don't forget that the next best point to make is why you want to join the new role, rather than leaving an air around your current (or impending) departure.

A nurse who interviews candidates frequently and read an early draft of this workbook had the following comment about avoiding negativity in interviews:

> *"On your 'angry-about-prior-job' point to readers…. Nursing encompasses millions of people, but each 'market' is a tiny little neck of the woods. None of us are more than six degrees of separation from your current boss, and that is sometimes even true across state lines. Experienced nurses that you are interviewing with have worked in the other systems, or if they haven't, their friends do. Few networks in other fields are as powerful as nursing networks. Never talk trash, even if your trash is true. Keep it brief and classy. It is effortless for us to find out what your immediate supervisor believes your weaknesses to be. Walk into the interview being aware of that."*

This interviewer made the further point that if your current boss is someone whose opinion she does not trust, she will already know to filter out or discount that information. In fact, rather than simply discounting it, she may even consider that you are doing a good job and that is why you have received criticism (e.g., your current boss could be jealous or obstructionist). Nursing is not the only field where networks are small, of course. Many interviewers have told me that they do not wait for an official list of references but already start calling people they know who can speak to a job candidate's character and ability to do the job, among other factors.

If in your heart of hearts you know that an informal reference check would *justifiably* put you in a bad light, you may wish to do some pro-active work to improve on points that have lead to consistent criticism in the past and find a way to let your network know that you have improved or turned over a new leaf.

Reputation management can take a lot of effort and may be difficult to pull off, but in some cases it is truly necessary.

__ I don't come across negatively

__ I need to work on getting past the negativity

Notes: _____

## H.   Don't *Over-Anticipate* Negative Questions

You may walk into an interview *knowing* that you will get asked a certain question that will be hard to answer with a smile on your face, and nonetheless the interviewer doesn't ask it. Some of us, in that situation, become extremely uncomfortable and feel the urge to "get it off our chest" anyway rather than give a more polished answer.

*Don't give into that feeling, as it is clearly the wrong approach.*

While you need to give an *authentic* answer to questions asked, this does not mean that you need to treat an interview like a confessional. Anything off track that will reflect negatively on you does not need to be said (although this does not mean that you should pretend not to understand or look for loopholes in what you are asked).

Even in response to a direct question, you do not need to *offer* more information than is required to give a sufficient, reasonable answer. Answer the question with sufficient details to set aside any concerns, and then move to a more positive topic or share (a tidy version of) what you have learned from the experience.

It is very likely that you will *not* be viewed as more honest due to your airing of dirty laundry, even if you pique the curiosity of the interviewer. You will instead be viewed as someone who does not know where to draw the line between professional and personal matters, and that is a dangerous and distracting personality to invite into one's office and onto one's team.

__ I have nothing to worry about here

__ I have something nagging at me and am afraid I will blurt it out

Notes: _____

## I.   Highlight Your Positive Points

While you do not need to offer unnecessary information about any *negative* points that your interviewer may have missed, you certainly want to create the opportunity to add *positive* points that your interviewer failed to ask. As I said above at the outset of this chapter, know your 3-5 main points that you want to get across, and find a way to work them into the conversation.

If all else fails, when you have an opportunity to ask questions, you can say, "I do have some questions, and I also want to make sure that I mentioned..." and then drive home your positive point(s).

__ I am ready to go on this front

__ I need to think more about the points I want to drive home

Notes: _____

**J.      Don't Talk Too Fast or Too Much**

If you are someone who talks too fast, or too much, you probably already know that you do it. You may also have an even greater tendency to do it in an interview, since you are nervous and hoping to make a good impression.

Instead, keep your answers to 2-3 sentences, don't rush and make sure to check in to see if the interviewer is still "with you." Don't break into a song and dance on a topic that the interviewer is not interested in hearing about, or doesn't understand, just because <u>you</u> feel more comfortable talking about it. Your comfort level is not the goal, even if it feels like that's a good place to be in the moment. If you need to choose between being comfortable and being hired, I suggest the latter.

Because I find this issue comes up quite often in practice interviews with clients, I am going to repeat my advice on this one at the risk of sounding redundant:

1)   Present in a logical progression whenever possible, and break your responses into manageable parts. For example, "I can tell you three ways that I have been proactive. First…." Now you have keyed the interviewer into the fact that he/she should be listening for three points, rather than wondering if your examples will never end. You have also given the interviewer tacit permission to ask questions after each one.

2)   Keep your answers short. Speak in 2-3 sentence blocks at most, unless something truly needs more time.

3)   Take a natural pause and check whether the interviewer is following the topic of conversation or instead looking down at his/her notepad, checking his/her watch, internally retreating into "won't you please stop talking?" land or otherwise.

4)   Ask if the interviewer wants to hear more about the topic you are discussing, e.g., "Should I go on…?"

*Coaching Moment*

*In a mock interview session coaching a private client, I asked the very first question of the interview, which was "tell me about the judge that you worked for?" In this case, she was a new graduate, and she had recently finished a clerkship in federal court.*

*My client launched into a non-stop, 10-sentence and three-and-a-half minute description of the judge and her impression of the court at which she had worked. (Yes, I was counting.) I took a time out at that point to let her know that this was an "icebreaker" question, just something to get her warmed up and start the conversation. My client had the disadvantage that we were conducting the interview by phone, so she could not see my expression, but in those cases an interviewee needs to pay even closer attention that the interviewer is still "with her" and actively listening. I had tried to break into her monologue, which she hadn't noticed, but could not because there were no gaps in her speech. A better alternative would have been to tell me 2-3 facts, pause and check if I had more questions.* **The art of the pause is underrated in interviews.**

\_\_ I don't do have this issue (and have confirmation from someone who has seen me in action in an interview or mock interview setting)

\_\_ I need to work on this

Notes: _____

## K.    Don't Get Off Topic or Overly Personal

One of the easiest ways to tank an interview is to forget that the interviewer is not your friend. Some interviewers may become your friends at some point in the future. Some may want to be your friend during the interview process, even giving some "friendly" advice. However, without appearing aloof or disinterested, you need to keep the train on the rails and stay focused on the "why should we hire you?" question.

This means that while you may (and should) bond over your mutual appreciation for cars, wine, travel, dogs, etc., don't take it over the line into a personal conversation. Follow the interviewer's lead. While it is safe to talk about how you loved a certain art museum in London that you visited while working abroad, you may be giving too much away if you discuss an extended backpacking trip through Vietnam (other than to mention it, if appropriate) and all of the places you visited while there.

The salient point is that common ground should build rapport but not take time away from your pitch about why you should be the one hired for the job.

*True-to-Life Example*

*You may be staying at your future in-laws house and had to take a shower at a neighbor's because their water was turned off. Your cat may have died that morning. You could be exhausted from a Bruce Springsteen concert the night before. None of these topics need to be discussed in your interview.*

*The only time a personal topic would need to be discussed in an interview is if you are so distraught emotionally that you are better off rescheduling. If that is the case, the more professional decision may be to actually reschedule – assuming you can give sufficient notice – than show up for an interview when you are not in the right mind. If a close family member has passed away, for example, most employers would not be offended to move the interview to the following week. You may pass up a job that way, but more likely you will not only fail the interview if you attend, but also sabotage your chances for working at the same company in the future, as well as increase the likelihood that you will feel negative about your general interviewing experience and ability to "do a good interview" if you proceed under highly stressed circumstances.*

\_\_ I don't come across this way

\_\_ I need to work on this

Notes: _____

**L.     Remember the Central Question:** *Why Should I Hire You?*

It bears repeating from prior chapters that every aspect of an interview involves the same underlying concern. The interviewer wants to know why he/she should hire you over the other candidates available. This is true regardless of the style of interview, whether you are being asked a question or making any form of presentation, from PowerPoint to a portfolio.

As Mark Stromberg, a partner at an architectural firm shared with me recently, he has taken to limiting an interviewee's portfolio time to 15 minutes. He then said:

> *Prior to instituting the time limit, candidates would show and discuss their portfolios in what seemed like a never-ending presentation. They were obviously very proud of their work and all of the details about what they had done. Yet I continued to be left with the question of how the work had benefited the company, and more importantly how they could benefit us. Many of them seemed to have a hard time getting to that point. Now, I give each candidate 15 minutes to present, and if he/she cannot get to the point within the timeframe, I know that he/she is not the right person to hire.*

If you tend to be one of those people who cannot get to the point – about why the words coming out of your mouth have any relevance to the interviewer's needs – I suggest you make a sign that says, "Why should you hire me?" with your top three answers and tape it to your bathroom mirror, so that you can see and be reminded of it the morning of your interview. At the same time, while you are presenting your portfolio or other work product (whether it is for 15 minutes or longer), don't forget to let your passion shine through. People want to hire people who enjoy their jobs, because they invariably make better employees and colleagues than the ones who don't.

__ I have internalized this point

__ I still need work getting to the answer to this question

Notes: _____

**M.     LEARN FROM PRIOR MISTAKES.**

If you have made any mistakes in interviews that have stuck with you – because you replay in your mind that very moment you (are certain that you) "lost" a job in the past – you may need to spend some time exorcising them.

The very act of "rewriting" your mistakes into positive actions can help you conquer fears about making a similar mistake in the future. However, it is not enough to identify your mistakes. You need to find alternative ways to act and turn them into habits, so that you do not fall back on the same set of errors.

For example, if you realize that in response to the question "tell me about yourself" you often give a five-minute answer without a break to make eye contact and check the interviewer is still engaged, it would not be enough for you to note that your answers are sometimes too long. What you would need to do instead is focus on the three main points to communicate that are relevant to the target role and figure out where and how you will pause to "check in" with your interviewer.

___ I have made mistakes in prior interviews that continue to haunt me

___ I don't dwell on or fear my mistakes; I have learned from them

The following workbook portions give you an opportunity to get your mistakes out of your head and onto the page, so that you can free yourself of them, if needed, as well as the chance to consider what you could have done instead, to be ready if a similar moment arises in a future interview.

Mistake #1

_____

_____

What I could have done differently (and can do in future interviews):

_____

_____

Mistake #2

_____

_____

What I could have done differently (and can do in future interviews):

_____

_____

Mistake #3

_____

_____

What I could have done differently (and can do in future interviews):

_____

_____

## N.    Create an Emotional Investment (Without Overdoing It)

If there is any professional means to create an emotional investment with your interviewer, you should find a way to do it. People hire people they like.

This does not mean name-dropping of someone you hardly know, but it does mean that if you have connections inside the company, share friends who are social with the interviewer, have common interests with the interviewer that he/she has made public (don't stalk them on a private Facebook account!) or otherwise are privy to some inside track, you should by all means find a convenient moment to mention it. For example: "I saw on your LinkedIn profile that you ran the Boston Marathon last year. I ran Chicago in 2014…."

If you have a friend or colleague in common, make sure that you have been in contact with the person recently and that he/she has a good impression of you (otherwise, don't mention it, as it is likely that the interviewer will get in touch with your common contact, whether or not he/she is an official reference).

It is easy to get back in touch with the common point of contact, by the way, even if you have not seen the person in a long time. Just mention that you are meeting with the interviewer about a possible job and ask whether your contact has any advice and his/her impression of the interviewer (as part of a polite, longer and heartfelt "catching-up" email or conversation). This helps with your diligence, makes you more prepared for the interview, gives you an "in" and is another opportunity to reconnect with your contact. A win on all accounts, in other words.

### True-to-Life Example

*Fifteen minutes into the interview, you may be asked a question that reveals you spent most of your childhood summers in Cape Cod, and it turns out that the interviewer spent summers there as well. You start reminiscing, finding that you know places and people in common. You learn that you both love oysters with a shot of Tabasco sauce, and together you have eaten enough to fill a boat. There's some playful banter and then a pause. The interviewer looks back at you. The ball is in your court. What do you say next?*

**Do you continue in the same vein or put the interview back on track about your skills and value proposition?**

*Not to put on any pressure, but the next words out of your mouth can make or break the interview.*

*Inside you are thinking "Score!" You have made a meaningful connection with the interviewer. After which you may think, "Sh\*t!" as you realize you have a significant choice to make about where to lead the interview next, and you do not know what to say.*

*Scan your interviewer for cues. Has he/she suddenly become all business? Is there room for another pass on the same topic that could serve as a segue to another point? Have you lost him/her for a moment altogether? (Maybe the interviewer has suddenly remembered that grandma is not doing well lately, and pretty soon they will need to sell that house with all of those childhood memories….)*

*Right here, at this moment, is why I consistently say that despite the best advice I or any other career expert can give you, we not in the room with you to coach you in "real time." What are you seeing across the table? You are in the midst of a conversation. What are the subtle cues across the table?*

*That said, I can tell you how to distinguish a good next line from a bad one. I have mentioned elsewhere in this workbook that you should not ask the compensation question in an interview. Here's a bad next line, and one that backhandedly goes to the compensation point:*

### *"Does the firm ever spring for oysters?"*

*Why doesn't this work? It is not the colloquial delivery, which is entirely appropriate. It is the directness of the question. This question makes it sound like you want to know whether your "living the life" experience from childhood will be replicated at the firm. It implies that you are interested more in what you will get out of the firm than what you can put into it. While I am not a judge of your true motives, I can tell you that coming across in an interview with an attitude of "what the firm can do for me" – whether or not you intend to sound that way – will not get you the job, unless you are in a truly tight market and only one of a few with your particular set of skills (e.g., a mechanical engineer with mining and project management experience interviewing for a job in the Canadian oil sands).*

*There's a simple way to turn the above question around and make it a positive one that bonds you with your interviewer, especially if you can deliver it credibly:*

### *"I bet you don't get a lot of that here, right?"*

*The word "that" in the sentence above refers to oysters, but also to the fun-in-the-sun days of youth. (I am assuming you are not applying to a lifestyle firm near the beach, in this case.) This form of question artfully turns the conversation back to business, while implying that you understand work is work. It also opens the door for your interviewer to offer more information in return, either a wistful "no, not really…" or a juicy "well, actually we do get [insert other benefit here]…." In either case, you win in the form of more information, maintaining the air of comradery and gently directing the conversation back to the task at hand. Most of all, you have not broken the mood or the emotional investment that the interviewer has made in you through the bonding moment. That **emotional investment** is what will carry the day later when the interviewer is trying to decide whom to hire or pitch to his/her fellow interviewing team, among a host of candidates, with only a pile of resumes and interview notes.*

__ I easily find ways to make connections with people

__ I need to work on how to make small talk, social niceties and points of connection (without overdoing it) in interview conversations

Notes: _____

## O.    Listen for Hidden Cues; Watch for Red Flags

For an astute interviewer, there are hidden clues everywhere about what it is like to work for an employer. Here are some examples:

- Are you taken to the coffee machine past the desks of some employees? If so, what is on their screens? Do they look happy, alert or slumped over in their desks? Is it a loud or quiet environment? Is it diverse?

- Are office doors generally open or closed?

- How do employees in the company interact with each other?

- In the interview itself, when you ask questions about the person who will be your direct superior or why the position has become available, for example, what is the interviewer's body language?

- Do the offices look upscale or rundown, and can you attribute this to the company being fiscally conservative, flashy, on the rise or barely making it?

- How quickly does the HR department or hiring manager respond to emails?

Make mental notes about what seems awry, if anything, or if it seems like your target company, department or team gets along exceptionally well. If there is anything that you think sends a "red flag," make sure to follow up on it later in the interview process, before accepting an offer.

Red flags I have noticed that I need to investigate and/or "clues" that I should consider:

1) Name of Employer:

_____

_____

Issues:

_____

_____

Plan to Investigate (e.g., follow-up questions, asking outside of the company):

_____

_____

2) Name of Employer:

_____

_____

Issues:

_____

_____

Plan to Investigate (e.g., follow-up questions, asking outside of the company):

_____

_____

You can make additional copies of the above as needed or find them on my blog at www.annemariesegal.com. (Click on "Worksheets.")

If you cannot follow up through conversations with people inside or outside of the company – and the inside conversations will need to be held with high discretion, preferably *after* your offer – you may be able to do some online research on the company to yield more data points for your decision. There is a range of sources, from Hoover's and Bloomberg to Vault and Quora, and each specific industry has its own wealth of information. As a start, you can search Google or another search engine for "company research tools," which will pull up a number of direct sources and links, as well as sites that instruct on how to conduct research on companies. You can also add specifics related to your search, such as "company research medical devices," to target relevant sources. This search result pulled up as a top hit, for example, Harvard Business School's Baker|Bloomberg Medical Devices Research Guide. See <http://www.library.hbs.edu/guides/meddevices.html>.

### A Job Seeker's Story

*"I can see now that I should have asked a lot more questions before I took this role. As it turns out, the company hires a lot of kids out of school, pays them almost nothing, works them 12 hours a day, gives them very little time to prepare or finish their work and sends them halfway around the state completing assignments.*

*At this point, I am so burned out. I can't tell if I should change fields or simply need a different job."*

### An Insider Story

*"Like dating, be careful that the image of the company is not a façade created for your benefit. The way our senior management actually runs our business doesn't correspond at all with the image that we present to the outside world. They look super organized and professional, and we are required to keep our desks clean in case of client visits. But honestly, they run around like crazy half the time and are always changing their minds midstream, with no coherency in their thought process or respect for employees' boundaries or contributions. I also hear them telling job candidates that they encourage employee interactions in the kitchen and common areas, but in reality you get nasty looks the minute*

*you are not sitting at your desk and working. In short, the brand doesn't match the reality.*
*You should really try to get the inside scoop before making a decision to work here."*

The second story above, while uncommon, is not exaggerated. Toxic work environments do exist, and we need to have our eyes and ears open during the interview process.

\_\_ I am on alert for (but not paranoid about) hidden cues from the employer

\_\_ I need to focus more on doing this in an interview

Notes: _____

## P.     Be Ready for Skype and Other Formats

There are many different formats of interviews, from traditional and phone to technology-enabled options and from pre-screening to full-panel interviews. Here are some examples of interview formats that you will see:

- **Pre-Interview** – This is like a stealth interview. You may get a call out of the blue and not even know that you are "interviewing" or you may have another meeting that turns into a pre-interview. Don't pick up the phone from a potential interviewing source, if you have any inkling who is calling, unless you are calm, focused and ready to have a business conversation.

- **Screening** – This is a short, formal meeting or call through which the company to determines whether it intends to interview you further. It is often conducted by human resources professionals or in-house recruiters who have a specific set of questions they want answered before they "green light" your candidacy.

- **Short Phone Interview** – Some early interviews are by phone and very short, in the range of 20 minutes. If you are told that you have been allotted 20 minutes, don't go over, but allow time in case the interviewer wants to speak longer.

- **Longer Phone Interview** – In longer phone interviews, you will have the same opportunities that you would at an in-person meeting to cover the interviewer's questions and ask your own, as they can last for an hour or more. Given the lack of non-verbal cues in a phone conversation, you will need to be very aware of how your voice sounds and whether you still have an interviewer's attention, if you get into a longer story or example. Phone interviews are difficult, as much as they may calm your nerves because you do not need to put on a suit. It is sometimes hard to read the interviewer's cues, because you cannot see their body language. Imperative for a phone interview is to have a good connection and no background noise. I have taken them in my car, on a (tested and) quiet street, a few blocks from my former office. If there's an unexpected sound, you can intermittently mute the line for a few seconds, or simply apologize that you looked for a quiet place near your office and did not expect the noise. Above all, stay focused, whatever happens.

- **Skype** – Skype allows you to interact more with your interviewer than is possible by phone. You should take care with setting up for a Skype interview, so that you convey a formality similar to an in-person setting. See more details below.

- **Panel** – Panel interviews may be expected or unexpected. If you are a senior candidate, you should be on notice that you may step into a panel interview at any time, whether it is with one or more people with whom you will be working or the CEO and/or Board of Directors. One of the keys to a successful panel interview is to make sure that you are addressing everyone in the room, not only the most senior people or the ones who are asking questions. It is often the person who appears to be least engaged in the conversation who is watching you most intently.

  The panel format is more often employed in second or third (or later) rounds of interviews, but be ready to adapt if you encounter it in your first round. The good news is that they consider you an important enough candidate to have more than one of their officers and employees take time out of their day to meet with you. Often you will get a list of names of interviewers whom you are expected to meet, but there can always be last-minute substitutions.

- **Take-home and other assignments** – Some companies opt to send assignments to candidates to complete, whether it is a sample problem, video presentation to create of themselves or otherwise. If you receive one of these requests, spend the time you need to get it right but also make sure to return it within the timeframe requested (or earlier, if possible).

- **Personality Tests** – Other companies prefer to offer tests created in-house or by a third-party vendor. While you want to be upbeat in your answers, of course, you also should not try to reverse engineer the questions, as consistency in responses is one of the traits for which they are testing (as otherwise it may appear you are being dishonest or trying to "game the test").

- **Lunch or Dinner** – Interviews over meals pose their own distinct challenges. You are evaluated on everything, including your table manners, interactions with the waitress and modulation of your voice. Your choice of conversation should be lighter than at the office, unless your interviewer continues to lead you into more substantive topics. As one job seeker put it, "They want to see if they would be happy to sit next to you for five hours on an airplane." This can be both metaphorical (do you fit with us?) and literal (would be a good travel companion?).

*More About Short Phone Interviews*

The key to any short interview is to prioritize. Have the main points (generally two or three) that you want to drive home and find a way to work them seamlessly into the conversation, have examples at the ready and prepare short, powerful follow-up questions. If you are successful at this stage, you will have more time to make a further presentation, so it's not optimum to try to fit everything into a short call.

Phone interviews do offer one distinct advantage over other formats. You can have your outlines in front of you, and it is easy to take notes. If available, I also like to print out (or have open online) a picture of the interviewer during the conversation, as I find it reminds me that I am talking directly to *that person* and not into the void.

*More About Skype*

Amanda Sherman, a financial executive and frequent interviewer, noted that Skype can present a particular problem for some candidates. Beyond checking that the lighting is optimum, the background is neutral or pleasing and you are dressed as you would for an in-person interview, you have technical issues to check beforehand. She recounted that:

> *"We recently interviewed four candidates over Skype. Three of them had tested their system the night before. The fourth had not, and his interview did not go well. We had such a hard time connecting with him that it was difficult to focus on the substance of the interview.*
>
> *If you are a student and your connection is bad in your dorm, go to an area of the library or another place where you can use Skype and the connection is strong. If you have nowhere to take a Skype interview, you should probably request to have a regular phone interview, which is better than having connection problems that detract from the meeting and, fair or not, can reflect poorly on you."*

*More About Interviews over Meals*

It sounds simple, but in truth a lack of table manners is a simple way to bomb your chances of being hired. Put your napkin in your lap, hold your fork properly and sit up straight in your chair. Make your mother and father proud, in other words. Look at your dining companions, don't order anything complicated or messy and eat at a reasonable pace.

I recall that in college, for example I met an international friend for dinner. While we were eating, he grabbed and ate a potato whole like an apple. I was so shocked that I said, "What are you *doing?*" He shot back, "What do you *mean?*" I had no idea that he (or anyone) normally ate that way – I thought he was playing around – and he in turn had never met someone who found this behavior out of the ordinary. Translating this situation to an interview context, follow what are considered good manners in the city and country where the interview is taking place (or international good manners, to the extent those exist), as international and regional differences may not reflect well on a job seeker.

___ I am prepared for different interview formats

___ I need to prepare further

Notes: _____

## Q.   Don't Rush the Process

As I have fleshed out in other places, you need to let the interview process proceed at the interviewer's pace. This means not getting ahead of yourself with questions that should be saved for a later point in the process, including compensation or benefits, and not becoming overly familiar with the individuals you meet during the course of your interviews. I would not connect with your interviewers on LinkedIn, for example, if you do not yet know whether you will be hired. (Although if you are turned down for a role and nonetheless had a strong rapport with a certain interviewer, you may decide to reach out at that time.)

There is one caveat to the general rule not to "rush" the pace of interviews, and this is when you have another offer pending. You may need to politely let your first choice employer know (as soon as possible, giving them the most time to respond) that you will soon need to make a decision about another role, and that it would be helpful to hear from them, if they are in the position to make a decision. The answer may be "no" on their end, but at least you have presented the opportunity.

__ I don't come across this way

__ I need to work on this

Notes: _____

## R.   Know How to Address Your Commute

This question comes up so often in interviews that it deserves its own section here. If you will have a long commute to your new office, especially if you are currently working closer to home, expect to be asked about it at some point during the interview process.

Employers are often suspicious of candidates with a long commute, especially if your drive or train/bus combination totals an hour or more (unless this is absolutely standard where you live). If you are one of the few Indiana or Wisconsin license plates in a parking lot full of cars from Illinois, for example, they may worry that you will bail if you find a job with a shorter commute and/or expect to work from home more often.

In many cases, these are valid concerns, so you should be honest with yourself about your commitment and (if you can do so truthfully) be ready to mitigate such concerns. Often the worst thing is not to pass on a job, but to accept the wrong job that becomes impossible to leave. A longer commute means you will place yourself further from future employers that are near your home – let alone local errands, childcare and home repairs – so the job needs to be worth it in order to make the tradeoff.

Some candidates try to address this concern by offering to move closer to the employer if they are offered the job. I would only suggest this if you have a very good "story" about why you intend to do that, and it does not sound as though the move is contingent on the employer. For example, if you have siblings, parents or a current or future spouse in the area and have been planning to move in any case. Otherwise, it may put too much pressure on employers to assure that a job works out for you – given what is at stake if it does not – which may discourage them from making the offer to avoid the situation altogether.

\_\_ I have a short commute or a ready answer for this question

\_\_ I need to prepare this answer

Notes: _____

## S.   Research Relocation and Be Ready to Discuss

As you may already be aware, some companies are willing to pay to relocate employees (and, if applicable, expenses such as licensing in the new jurisdiction), while others do not have the approval or budget to do this. In some ways, the discussion is akin to the one about compensation: you may not want to be the first one to address whether they will cover your costs, because you may be unnecessarily giving something away if you imply that you will pay for relocation yourself. You should assume that, if you are already in the interview room and they have not already addressed the point in a pre-screening, the chance they will relocate you is likely (but not certain).

Outside of the issue about who will pay for relocation, you should show an interest in the region, city or town to which you will be relocating, knowledge of the area and, if possible, connections through family, friends or frequent travel there or nearby. (It is also helpful to establish this relationship in your cover letter, when you send in your initial application.)

In addition, be ready for regional differences in compensation, which may be brought up initially or part of the negotiation process. You may be coming from a locale that pays more or less, and you need to be aware of whether you will be treated like an "expat" and paid according to your home location or your salary will be adjusted to what the locals earn.

In some locations, the salary can be lower as a matter of course, because demand is high and supply is low for jobs in the area, such as Colorado and Florida's so-called "Sunshine Tax." In others, you should expect to be paid more.

Senior candidates have more at stake in compensation and benefits packages, and this is often a reason to have a recruiter or other experienced professional – who knows the market – help you get your best package or manage your expectations (if needed).

\_\_ I am familiar with my target market and ready to discuss relocation

\_\_ I still need help with how to have this conversation

Notes: _____

## T.    Know How to Address Potential Bias or Illegal Questions

Interviews are fraught with the opportunity for bias, intentional or not, and illegal questions. For interviews in the U.S., a good place to start finding information is on the EEOC's website. See, for example, <https://www.eeoc.gov/laws/practices>.

To sum up (and please check official sources for the current laws), here is what is covered: With limited exceptions, any questions that reveal your age, race, national origin, gender, religion, marital status and sexual orientation are off-limits for any covered employers. So are certain protected categories, such as national origin, citizenship, age, marital status, disabilities, arrest and conviction record, military discharge status, race, gender identity, pregnancy status or genetic information. That said, if any of these questions relate directly to specific occupational qualifications – i.e., are integral to the job you will be doing – they may be legitimate and not a breach of federal or state discrimination laws.

Illegal questions can come up more often than you might expect. Declining to answer a question is one possible response, although at times it may cost you the opportunity. Another possibility is to deflect the question or politely change the subject to a new or related topic. Even the most careful, open and unbiased interviewer can make mistakes, and he/she may quickly catch the error and be grateful that you have not drawn attention to it. If your interviewer persists and you start to feel uncomfortable, you can say graciously, "Please help me understand why my answer is important for the role, so I can know better how to respond to your question."

Illegal questions and bias may also come up in unique ways, and in some cases what sounds like bias may not be intended as such. Your interview may ask, "Hmm…. Is that a Persian name?" The interviewer could be negatively typecasting you, or his/her next words may be, "That's wonderful. My [grandmother/best friend/husband/etc.] is from Persia. [She/he] makes the best tahdig …." with the question being not one of bias but intended to make a connection.  While the question may be illegal under U.S. law, the person asking it could have an entirely innocent motive (and be, at the moment, oblivious to the error). It is up to you to decide how to respond.

In this complex and diverse world, my practical advice to most candidates is to be who you are and know that a biased interviewer (if he/she represents the mood of the employer) would not be a good fit. For certain job seekers, however, especially those who have been unemployed for long periods of time and suspect bias may be at play, it may be appropriate to take a different approach. Further, if you are subject to continual bias in your job search, you may decide that the best remedy (and alternative to alleging discrimination or continuing the good fight, which, although important, can be a source of negative energy for job seekers) is to move to a more cosmopolitan geographical location, industry or field where discrimination is less prevalent.

Of course, bias is not only about illegal questions, it is also about respecting others. If you happen to be an interviewer at times (and not only a job seeker) and want to do a better job of showing that respect, DiversityInc – sponsored by a number of Fortune 500 and other major companies – has a great site with examples of "what not to say" to candidates or in the workplace generally. See <http://www.diversityinc.com/topic/things-not-to-say>.

Note that each jurisdiction has its own laws, so the above illegal questions relate generally to the U.S. job market, but this is not a full discussion of the facts that may apply to your situation. Consult an employment lawyer and/or do your own research if you have any concerns that you have been treated unfairly or improperly under the law. In addition, if the bias arises <u>after</u> you have taken your new job, you may wish or need to consider what remedies may be appropriate.

___ I am comfortable in an interview where I may face bias or illegal questions

___ I still need help with turning those conversations around or, failing that, exiting gracefully

Notes: _____

## U.    Be Prepared to Discuss Compensation, if Asked

It is not uncommon for recruiters (and sometimes interviewers) to ask salary requirements upfront, although the recent prohibition in Massachusetts barring employers from asking these questions may be followed by other states. If you are asked about your salary requirements, and you *know* that your bottom line is out of the usual range for a role, you may wish to mention this upfront rather than proceed through the process, only to pass on the opportunity because they could not afford you (or would not increase the compensation to meet your requirements). That said, it is often better to couch these conversation in terms of the "total compensation package" rather than have everything ride on a number, unless your base salary is something on which you cannot or will not compromise.

If you are more flexible about what you are willing to accept, it is often a prudent approach to ask further questions about compensation rather than responding first, and to give a range when pressed. For example, "Could you give me a sense of what you are contemplating to pay the successful hire…?" puts the ball in their court.

It may be, however, that you cannot avoid being the first to show your hand, and some interviewers want to have this conversation upfront, even as early as the screening interview. I would be ready to give an answer at the outset of the process, if needed, rather than sound as though you have not given it enough thought or are not decisive about what you want and need to be paid.

If the new role will be sufficiently different from what you have done before (in scope or seniority, for example), you may not yet know what compensation makes sense. In some cases, the best answer may be, "I am still trying to get my arms around [i.e., understand] what this new role will entail, and I am not ready yet to commit to a number. What did you have in mind?"

___ I know my bottom line and am comfortable having salary discussions when needed

___ I still need help with how to have this conversation

Notes: _____

## V.      Don't Sound Like a Pompous You-Know-What

I wish I could say "enough said" with the title to this subsection, but the truth is that if you sound like a pompous you-know-what in interviews, the only plausible reason (other than pure and total narcissism) is that you have no idea you are coming across that way. It may come from nerves, or it may be for another reason, but instead of projecting an image of confidence, you may be projecting condescension, annoyance or other unflattering qualities.

So what does it mean to sound like a pompous you-know-what? Generally, it means that you sound as though the interviewer is wasting your time or asking you questions that are "beneath" you or that he/she is less knowledgeable about certain topics than you are. This may happen when an interviewer asks an open-ended question, such as "how much experience do you have with [name of programming language or other substantive competence]?" If you feel inwardly offended that you are asked to demonstrate your knowledge rather than grateful that you have a chance to shine, this may come across in the interview. Don't talk down to the interviewer, even if he/she is very junior to you or a non-technical person interviewing for a technical role. If you cannot come across as someone who can communicate without condescension, it is likely that you will not be hired.

### True-to-Life Example

*Imagine that your interviewer asks if you are familiar with Section 501(b) of a certain regulation. In your mind, you know that Section 501(b) is the law, while the implementing regulation is 5.01b(5). You may be wondering if this is a test. Is your interviewer trying to quiz you on whether you know the difference? Should you correct the interviewer or ignore it?*

*Don't overthink it. Remember, the interview is not about what you want, it is about what you can do for the employer. Yes, there may be a few interviewers who are actually trying to test you, but most of them are not. In either case, your answer should be the same. You say, "Right, 501(b)..." and move on to your familiarity with it. At the same time, nod at the interviewer to imply that you understood this is what he/she meant.*

*Compare this to saying "Do you mean the law or the regulation?" This forces the interviewer into the uncomfortable position of saying, "yes, I actually meant the law" or trying to one-up you in return. Imagine that you did this on a regular basis at work. You would not be very popular. No one cares about these minor details, except when they affect outcomes.*

*Remember, it's not racquetball; it's a friendly game of Ping-Pong. The goal is to volley, not crush your opponent. We all know this instinctively, but in the moment, some of us forget.*

Another way to sound like a pompous you-know-what is to talk too much about yourself. Again, you may not actually *be* pompous, but you can nonetheless come across that way if you are not careful. To return to the example above, if you are asked about your experience with 5.01b(5), and you answer, "yes, I have *extensive* experience" and proceed to give the interviewer a three-minute monologue about it, you are unlikely to come across as careful and knowledgeable but instead convey an air of self-importance. If you feel it is important to give significant details about your knowledge of a particular substantive area, whether legal, technical or otherwise, the way to do it is to give some high-level information first and then ask if the interviewer wants to hear more.

### *In My Experience: Vet Your Referral Candidates Well*

*I emphasize the point above, about not appearing pompous, for two reasons. The first, as I mentioned, is that you may fall into this trap unnecessarily. The second is that this particular type of feedback is difficult to give, so even if you have received "critiques" of your interview style in the past, you may not have been given the full feedback necessary to tone it down (or you may not have demonstrated this style in an obvious way, especially if the people helping you with practice interviews know you well and/or can speak "at your level" with regards to subject matter discussed). In many fields, you can recover from a host of interview offenses, but you can never recover from the taint of appearing pompous (unless you end up working for someone with a high tolerance for it, which only works until you cross the line).*

*I remember clearly, although it was over eight years ago, recommending a colleague and friend (let's call him George) for a position with a former employer of mine. George would have come in at a level similar to mine, held the "perfect resume" for the position and already knew a number of us. Nonetheless, of the other people who interviewed him, at least two thought George came across as pompous. These were partners of the firm, whose opinions (frankly) mattered more than mine. They peppered me with examples of how George had come across as condescending and openly worried that he would act that way on deals, not to mention annoy and offend senior management of the firm. It was clear to them that, George's credentialed and well-suited background notwithstanding, he would never be a fit for our firm. He would have been bounced out the door in five days, if not five minutes, the first time he offended someone important and tarnished a relationship that had taken years to build.*

*So we hired someone else who had analogous (but no direct) experience in the field and I was stuck telling George why he did not get the job. I must admit that I never gave him the real reason. How can you tell a friend, "they thought you were kind of a jerk, but otherwise you probably would have gotten the job..."? It doesn't bode well for a continued professional relationship, let alone a friendship. Worse yet, George and I slowly fell out of touch after that.*

__ I don't sound pompous at all, why are you even writing this?

__ I don't think that I have this problem (do I?)

Notes: _____

## W.   CLOSE THE DEAL.

Toward the end of the interview, look for a good time to ask about next steps. This may be, for example, the last of your follow-up questions. You want leave the interviewer with a positive impression and indication of your interest (if, in fact, that is accurate), and you can ask about next steps in the process, if they still have a number of candidates to interview and other innocuous questions that help provide clarity and direction.

You may also wish to ask what follow-up on your end is appropriate. For example, you could say: "So I understand you expect it may be two or three weeks until I hear back. Should I follow up at that point if I haven't received a call?" Your goal is not to push, of course, but to pave a path for continued communication and let the interviewer know that you are pro-active and results-oriented.

\_\_ I know how to close

\_\_ I know that I need to work on this

Notes: _____

Of the points in this chapter, my greatest challenges are:

_____

_____

_____

My plans to address these challenges are:

_____

_____

_____

_____

_____

Other points that I want to remember are:

_____

_____

_____

_____

_____

# PART 5:

# FINAL CONSIDERATIONS

# CHAPTER 13
# BREAKING THROUGH INTERVIEW BLOCKS AND RAISING YOUR CONFIDENCE

*"I truly hate my job, but I can't face the idea of going to an interview."*
- Senior Hedge Fund Operations Professional

*"I admit I am stuck. But I can't seem to get myself out of it."*
- Career Changer

Interviews are hard. There is no denying it. So hard that sometimes they cause some of us to stay in jobs that no longer make sense for us or even cause us serious psychological or physical pain.

Let's start with the small things. Not only do we hate having to "dress to impress" and all the fancy footwork that goes with it, but we also hate worrying whether these items of clothing will make it through to the end of the interview intact. There are a thousand other little worries – from our boss knowing we are job-hunting to having to revise our resumes to even get a foot in the door – that can make interviewing an unbearable prospect.

The unique challenges of job search and interviewing can **keep you stuck** in a job you no longer want or, worse yet, unemployed or unable to return to the workplace after a period of absence. Meanwhile, if you don't address the fear or other concerns that may compel you to keep the interview process at bay or perform at less than your best, you will lose great opportunities for better jobs, more compensation, greater connection to your employer, friendlier co-workers and the like.

If you are one of the people who hates interviews and your aversion is holding you back, the most important investment you can make in yourself is to face your fears and improve your interviewing skills.

Here are nine fundamental reasons someone may absolutely loath (or fear) interviews, one or more of which may apply to you. Feel free to circle or underline any that jump off the page at you, and add any secret fears (that you do not need to share beyond your notes in this book, unless you believe sharing will help you conquer them).

If you are fortunate not to suffer any of the blocks below and don't need any of the confidence-builders on the pages in this chapter, cheers to you. You can skip to Chapter 14. Otherwise, let's address these points so you can break free of the blocks.

## A.    Nine Common Blocks

Common interview blocks, of which you may have one or more, include:

1)   **POWERLESSNESS.** Interviews can make us feel powerless, unable to control the course of the meeting or outcome.

2)   **FEAR OF FAILURE TO MEASURE UP.** Interviews require us to take an objective look at what we have accomplished in our careers to date or admit things, such as our weaknesses. We can fear that we won't "measure up" to our own expectations or those of others.

3)   **FEAR OF REJECTION OR AVERSION TO PROVING OURSELVES.** We may fear rejection, even if we are non-committal about a specific job or company. We also may not want to "jump through hoops" in order to get a new job.

4)   **OPPORTUNITY COSTS.** We often don't want to invest the time in multiple interviews, because we fear missing out on other things we could be doing with the time, including performing in our current jobs.

5)   **PRESSURE OR PANIC.** We know that even if we are, in fact, the best candidate for a certain role, we might "blow our chance" if we make one fatal mistake in an interview, and we don't want that kind of pressure.

Sometimes this pressure rises to the level of panic. Interviews can send us into a tailspin – dizziness, shortness of breath, etc. – if we start to ruminate about what will happen if we remain stuck in our current situation, let a fear of change run wild or have a disposition that is prone to panic and have not learned a way to cope.

6)   **SHELLSHOCK.** If we have been in a toxic work environment (or continue to be in one), we may be distrustful of <u>any</u> future job situation, making it difficult to perform well in an interview.

7)   **LACK OF PRESENTATION SKILLS.** We can't always express ourselves as well as we would like or are afraid we will get tripped up or be unable to convey our most important points.

8)   **UNFAMILIARITY WITH THE PROCESS.** We may feel like there is a set of ground rules in the interview process that we don't fully understand, or the process may not unfold in the manner that was initially explained.

9)   **PRIOR FAILURES.** If we have not achieved success in prior interviews, we may find it difficult to ready ourselves to interview again.

As I read through the nine points above and reflect on my thoughts, I realize that my greatest causes of blocks and stress in the interview process are:

_____

_____

_____

My initial thoughts about how to overcome these stressors:

_____

_____

_____

People, places and things that can help me cope with and/or move beyond the blocks and/or stress:

_____

_____

_____

Themes I can recognize about my stressors:

_____

_____

_____

## B.    Overcoming the Blocks

Let's return to each of the nine blocks discussed at the outset of this chapter and discuss some possible solutions to each concern. If you feel that after reading the points below you need further work to get through your blocks, you may wish to consider working with a career transition coach, getting assistance from the career center at your university, asking a trusted friend for help or (if the issues run very deep) seeking professional guidance.

1)    POWERLESSNESS.

*How to overcome it:*

Treat the interview like a two-way street. You ultimately have the power to say "yes" or "no" to each stage of the process and to a job offer in the same way that the company has the power to run the interview and extend an offer or not.

*Example:* You may have a "flaky" interviewer who keeps rescheduling appointments at the last minute, asking you to come in on short notice and/or falling out of touch for long periods of time. You have control not only over your literal response (while remaining professional, of course) – "sorry, I am not free this Thursday, but I am free Friday or Monday" – but also over your emotional response.

It is important not to ignore that second factor, your emotional response, in these situations. Often, we don't face the fact that we need to find a new job until the last possible moment, among other reasons because we don't want to have to manage all the factors that go into a transition, so our job search can become an act of desperation. When we get to that point, we can overvalue the input of recruiters, hiring personnel and interviewers, as if our life's fate is in their hands. It is not.

*"The best advice my father ever gave me is that in an interview, I am interviewing them just as much as they are interviewing me. I was in my late 30s before I understood what he meant. I would have saved so much stress if I had just believed him in my 20s. He also told me that every interview is practice, another concept I also did not understand at the time. Now in my 40s, I actually love interviews. It's exciting and fun to meet new people. And if it isn't, I don't want that job. It was a nice conversation that sharpened my interviewing skills. No harm, no foul."*
-Seasoned interviewer and occasional job seeker

2)    FEAR OF FAILURE TO MEASURE UP.

*How to overcome it:*

If you fear that you will not measure up to an interviewer's expectations, likely you need to take a hard look at whether you have a perfectionist streak or otherwise do not measure up to your own. Often, we are our own harshest critics, and we seek assurances from others that validate feelings we already have (whether or not these feelings make sense; there is comfort in the familiar). An interviewer whom you have never met should not have enough importance in your life for you to worry whether you will be "worthy" of a certain role or advancement. Learn to appreciate your own worth, and others will recognize that you are exactly at the right place on your path.

If you feel that you have not had the career to this point that you wish you had, the only way out of that is to move forward.

3)    FEAR OF REJECTION OR AVERSION TO PROVING OURSELVES.

*How to overcome fear or rejection:*

I see fear of rejection come up often with, for example, back to work candidates who have been away from a professional context for a number of years or older job seekers who are having a hard time finding a suitable replacement role (or, sometimes, any role) after a significant layoff. Remember that everyone has been rejected for a job at one point or failed to reach another outcome in their professional career that they coveted dearly, even the person sitting in the interviewer's shoes. (And if you are interviewing with the rare someone who has never faced this eventuality, it can only mean they have not had "stretch goals" or taken appropriate risks.) Rejection is a strong word, and failing to secure a job for which you have interviewed is not necessarily "rejection," just a failed match.

Here as everywhere, the old cliché is true: nothing ventured is nothing gained. The more interviews you undertake (for jobs that make sense at this point in your career), the better your chances of finding the right fit. Rather than viewing a failed match as a setback, just continue to roll the dice (while improving your skills and vision each time, learning from experience) until your numbers come up. It only takes one offer to get a job.

*How to overcome aversion to proving oneself:*

If you feel that you have already "made it" in your career and do not want to jump through hoops, I hear you. What I suggest in this case is to approach the interview as an information and opportunity exchange rather than a meeting between interviewer and interviewee. Only accept those interviews that will allow you to approach them on equal footing. This does not mean you can be unresponsive or abrupt, but it does mean that you can approach the interview as one that is designed to ascertain mutual benefit and fit rather than a test of your worthiness for a role. At a certain point in your career, the attitude that "none of us want to waste anyone's time, so let's only proceed if it makes sense for both of us…" is not only acceptable, but in fact it makes for an attractive candidate.

4)   OPPORTUNITY COSTS.

*How to overcome this concern:*

If you are worried that going to interviews is a "waste of time" because you never seem to get the role you want, you can start to become concerned about opportunity costs and look for a way to be smarter about how you spend your time. I applaud you for this decision but do not suggest that you stop interviewing as a result.

Every activity must be valued based on our priorities and what else we must give up instead in order to complete it. If you are overly concerned about opportunity costs, ask yourself if there is a reason that your interviews are not resulting as intended and seek to fix the problem, rather than avoiding interviews altogether. Are you presenting yourself right? Are you going for the right roles in the first place?

In addition, as I mentioned above, much of the work to prepare for an interview is also helpful to reflect on your current role, company, growth opportunities and career path generally. Interviewing therefore does double-duty, helping you know what is "out there" in the market as well as giving you an opportunity to look more objectively at your current job situation. Remember, staying at the same place is as much of a decision as making a change, especially with the amount of mobility available in most jobs today.

5)   PRESSURE OR PANIC.

*How to overcome the feeling of pressure:*

If you are feeling pressure (that does not rise to panic, covered below), there are a few cures that can help. The first is to take time for preparation: know your value proposition and fit with the company, answers to tough questions, plan for interview day, etc. Have your suit ready to go, and get your route to the interview down. Print out anything you may need for the interview (see "Bring Backup" in Chapter 11 above) and slip it into a folder that is filed in a safe place.

The second is to de-stress, whether your means to do that is yoga, running, kickboxing, music, gardening, tea, wine, chocolate or something else altogether.

On the subject of food and drink, proper nutrition is important to keep your energy levels up, especially the morning of the interview. Protein is a must, and it's best to avoid any foods that don't sit well with you. This is not the time to be adventurous; save your culinary risk-taking for the celebratory dinner.

In addition, if you are loyal to your current boss or have another reason that you may not accept your new job, and this is part of the cause of your stress, you may need to practice the art of compartmentalizing for purposes of the interview. Even if you are of "two minds" about whether you will actually leave your current job – a point to consider later as you evaluate your options – you will do best to approach the interview with an open mindset rather than let your thoughts and judgment be clouded with concerns.

*How to overcome panic:*

If you experience panic in the context of interviews (or one interview in particular), rather than mere pressure as I discuss above, I suggest working with a career coach or other professional who has experience with candidates in this situation. Likely there are many moving pieces in your life that threaten to collide, and you may even have physical or psychological elements that contribute to your state of mind.

One important point to identify is what may be causing the panic and try to ascertain whether the fear is based on actual triggers or perceived concerns, and in either case what can mitigate such trigger or fear. For example, you may feel panic that your current boss will find out that you are interviewing and therefore be unable to concentrate in the interview, only focused on your worry that you will lose your job.

Finally, visualization techniques can help you imagine succeeding and thereby achieve success.

If your panic is debilitating or extends into other aspects of your life, seek help beyond the scope of this book.

6)    SHELLSHOCK.

*How to overcome shellshock:*

If you currently work in a toxic environment, where colleagues cannot be trusted, micromanagement is a sport and/or negativity pervades, the main cure is to get out more. You need meaningful social and professional contacts outside of the workplace to maintain perspective. In addition, you may need to have a number of interviews to become familiar with different work environments, so that you know better what you are looking for. You will also benefit from my advice in earlier chapters to "interview back" – i.e., get all of your questions answered and make sure that you conduct sufficient due diligence before making a decision. As you finish each interview, be sure to complete the debriefing form (or a variation of it) in Chapter 16 so that you can compare notes across roles.

7)   LACK OF PRESENTATION SKILLS.

*How to overcome it:*

There are a number of ways to overcome a lack of presentation skills, including (of course) reading this and other books on interviewing. One obvious way is to practice not only interviewing but other forms of "performing" outside your comfort zone. Note, however, that you will only seriously improve if you find a way to get outside feedback during the process. Otherwise, you risk making the same mistakes time and again rather than learning how to fix them.

8)   UNFAMILIARITY WITH THE PROCESS.

*How to overcome it:*

This one is generally pretty easy to overcome. Read this book and other books like it. Ask questions of people who have done it before. Practice. Interview a lot. It gets easier as time goes on.

If you are interviewing in a new field or industry and are unfamiliar with how those interviews are conducted, find someone through your network who can give you the inside story.

In addition, if you are a new graduate, you might seek out books that explain "how the work world works," such as *They Don't Teach Corporate in College* by Alexandra Levit. If you are very senior in your career and want to know how to break through to true leadership, you can read Dorie Clark's *Stand Out* or Seth Godin's *Linchpin*, among other titles. The Harvard Business Review's website, magazine and press also have a range of helpful topics that are always insightful.

9)   PRIOR FAILURES.

*How to overcome them:*

Look forward, not back.

Review your prior mistakes (there is a workbook portion devoted to this review in Chapter 12), but don't dwell on them. If you can devise how you would have "fixed" each mistake, you can retrain your brain to avoid the mistake in the future. Remember, you are *complete and whole*, and certainly bigger than any prior mistake.

Find your favorite mantras or song lyrics, and get yourself in the right frame of mind to make this next interview your best one.

My plan to address my stressors before/in the next interview is:

_____

_____

_____

When I master these points, my life will be different because:

_____

_____

_____

_____

## C.      Confidence-Building

In previous chapters, I discussed the basic elements of how to define your value proposition in an interview. You cannot properly envision your value proposition, however, if you lack the self-confidence to appreciate the value you add.

There are two necessary elements in the confidence equation. First, you need to build confidence. Second, you need to maintain confidence over time.

(Note: for those of you who have no issues with self-confidence whatsoever, go ahead, skip to Chapter 5. Although you probably didn't need me to tell you that!)

*"Just Be Confident"*

A couple of years prior to becoming a coach, I completed a yoga teacher training. One of my most important insights from the program was the simple fact that *you cannot teach someone to relax by telling them to relax.* If you have ever thought about it, you quickly realize that it is true. You cannot convince a spouse, student, child parent or anyone else to relax simply by saying the words, "Relax." Don't believe me? Give it a try.

Instead of telling someone to relax, you will inspire much greater ease if you create an environment that is relaxing, inspire a state of trust so the individual can let go of whatever is holding him/her back and give specific instructions about how he/she can enter a state of relaxation (e.g., take slow inhalations and exhalations to the count of 10 or tighten your hands into a ball and then slowly loosen your grip, noticing if anything shifts as you do so).

Inspiring confidence works the same way. You cannot "make" someone feel more confident simply by saying, "Be confident. You'll do great." If I want to help you grow your confidence, I need to give you specific tools to get you there and a perspective that allows the confidence to blossom on its own.

I would venture to say that most (probably all) of us have situations in which we feel more or less confident, and lack of confidence is greater among those who have do not believe they have met some external or internal bar set for themselves. Even if things seem to come easy for some people, they may lack confidence when asked to perform above the level to which they are accustomed or in new environments, because they fear failure (whether or not they recognize it as such).

This "setting of a high bar" means that a former financial analyst who has been out of the job market for 10 years and wants to return may no longer feel confident because she still has the same high expectations of herself, which she wants to meet (and thinks everyone else will want her to meet, whether or not they knew her before) on the very first day back to the job. It also means that someone who has made great strides as a Chief Financial Officer of a thriving public company could nonetheless lack confidence to serve as its Chief Executive Officer and/or Chairman of the Board. At the same time, those who are less risk adverse and more willing to step out of their comfort zones, or simply learn from mistakes without dwelling on them, may be able to step into either of these roles without fear. Whether they would be better at the job is another matter, but lack of confidence would not hold them back.

So how do we get comfortable <u>moving out of our usual comfort zones</u>, so we are just as confident stating our value proposition at a job interview as we are ordering a tall double shot soy latte with extra foam and stating our name to be written on a paper cup? (Starbucks-speak does not come naturally, you must admit.) Here are some ideas to increase your confidence in the interviewing context:

1) Focus on serving others' needs rather than your own anxiety.

2) Look at the larger picture.

3) Remove externalities, such as your estimation of what the interviewer thinks of you (often based on how you are perceived in your current role).

*Know Your Value*

If you feel your confidence slipping at any point, go back and review your value proposition and lists of accomplishments from Part 2 of this workbook. In addition, go on informational interviews and talk with people in your field who can help you get back in the right mindset to remember exactly why you are so amazing at what you do.

When you need more support, ask someone who knows you on a professional level to help you get further insights into your value. Sometimes others can see what we cannot see ourselves.

*Dump the Downers*

If you are having a confidence slump, remove people from your life to the extent possible (and make it possible) who always bring you down. You can always invite them back, if you still want to do that, after your job search is completed. If you hear negative thoughts, you may internalize them.

If you cannot remove people from your life, screen out their comments as personal opinions (not fact) and as small nagging voices or background noise (not important input).

*Get a Haircut (or an Image Consultant)*

Appearance plays a big part in how we perceive ourselves. Maybe your confidence needs a boost by updating or enhancing your personal brand through your image. If it helps and you have an ability to invest in yourself, consider an image consultant to streamline your personal presentation and wardrobe. Failing that, a new suit, shoes or haircut can change your mood for the better and help you feel recharged and ready to take on the next challenge.

If you have greater challenges, such as weight or health concerns, or depression, focus on getting yourself to where you want to be, and don't wait to address these until you are in your new role. Change management is hard at any stage in our lives, and often there is the "excuse" that everything will be better once you are settled into a new home, job, relationship, etc. Sometimes, the change that needs to happen in the rest of your life is what will allow your job search to go forward.

*Get a Life*

Confidence is not a quality that, once acquired, stays with us forever. We may have confidence right out of the gate, when looking for a new role or otherwise, but over time we find that our confidence degrades. We start to second-guess ourselves or receive what is obviously or arguably negative feedback during the interview process. We then become like someone who is swimming to shore while out at sea, with the shore seeming to move farther away with each successive stroke. If only we got a glimpse that we were making progress, it would help us gather that burst of energy, commonly called a second (or third or fourth) wind, to keep us going.

To maintain confidence, one of the best things you can do is "get out of your own way." As part of this process, do not focus on your job search 24/7. It will only make you more paranoid each day that you *still* do not have a new job. Job search on a regular schedule, e.g., 9 am–3 pm three or five days a week (including informational interviews), 25 flexible but carefully tracked hours each week or (if you are still currently employed or addressing "life concerns") the greatest amount of time you can reasonably devote. In the meantime, get to the gym, go rock climbing, visit a waterfall or desert, play piano, write a blog or do whatever else makes you enjoy life. You will be a more energized and compelling candidate if you come across rested, energized and happy rather than wound up, discouraged and tense.

*Coaching Moment*

*A client who has a job (but needs a change) and had been actively searching for a new role for months admitted to me recently that she had spent the last two weekends water skiing rather than using every available opportunity for her job search. She asked sheepishly if that was OK, and I told her it was fantastic. You can't make good progress if you don't take breaks once in a while.*

*In addition, maybe one of those water skiing trips includes a family friend who has the perfect job and will be open and available to discuss it. You never know.*

If you have a tendency to self-sabotage or get "blocked," what can you do to prepare yourself beforehand?

_____

_____

What do you most need to work on in interviewing?

_____

_____

How can you work on that further?

_____

_____

How can you project confidence in the interview?

_____

_____

What problems do you most like to solve?

_____

_____

What type of work environment best suits you?

_____

_____

# CHAPTER 14
# ADDRESSING SPECIAL CONSIDERATIONS IN YOUR CANDIDACY

## A.     You Are Underqualified

Sometimes job seekers apply for various roles at a company in which they are interested, on the hopes that if they are not qualified for a certain role at a certain level, they will be a match for another opportunity. Interviewers may call in candidates on the same assumption.

If you have been called for an interview, assume you are qualified for the position, unless that assumption is called into question by the interviewer. At that point, depending on the circumstances, tone of the interview and other factors, you need to make a quick decision how to approach such a question. My advice would be not to answer with a "yes" or "no" but rather go through the list of requirements. For example, you may say, "I saw that the job description asks for someone with experience working in [X]. I have been doing that for six months, and in that time I have accomplished...." This turns the discussion away from an open and shut judgment about whether you are qualified and toward the value you can bring. You still may be judged as not having enough experience, but you increase your odds of being hired if you start from a place of confidence rather than self-doubt.

Notes: _____

## B.     You Are Overqualified

If you are concerned that you will be viewed as overqualified or have received this feedback in the past, you are probably frustrated at perceived (or actual) discrimination. Common situations in which this happens are, for example, if you need to take a role that is a step-down in your title or responsibilities, or if you are highly educated or had a high-level job but have been on an extended leave and want to get back into the workforce.

To be ready for the next interview, it is helpful to contemplate concerns an employer may have, for example:

1)   You will be too expensive.
2)   You will have an "inflated" sense of self-worth.
3)   You will be inflexible.
4)   You will be bored.
5)   You will leave as soon as a "better" opportunity comes along.
6)   You can (and may) take his/her job.
7)   You see the job as a semi-retirement strategy.

I would be ready, if you expect you may raise a question in this regard, to demonstrate you are savvy to the concerns above. In the case of flexibility, for example, show how that you have kept up your skills, talk about how you demonstrated flexibility in certain situations and above all come across as flexible to your interviewer rather than someone who needs to "drive" the conversation or process. To combat a perception that you may be too expensive, you can emphasize that you are willing to pitch in where needed and do not have an attachment to titles or seniority levels (a proxy for compensation).

If the reason you are considering the role is because you need a "lower stress alternative" than your prior job, by all means you can say that, but make sure to couch it in professional terms rather than make excuses for it. "At this point in my life, I value [X] over [Y]...."

As one interviewer conveyed to me:

> *"When I open the interview with a 'tell me about yourself' type question, don't ever tell me that you're an 'old hand at this' and you've 'done everything and seen everything.'*
>
> *I'm not going to hire someone who's already bored three minutes into the interview. I'm not being ageist. I want someone who's interested."*

The good news is that you are 100% qualified. Remember that, because it means that you *still* have an edge, if you can address the interviewer's concerns as mentioned above.

How can I be ready to address any concerns about my candidacy?

1) _____

_____

2) _____

_____

3) _____

_____

## C.   You Are a Career Changer (and Don't Yet Fit the "Call" of the Job)

If you are changing careers or still establishing yourself in your chosen field (which is itself a career transformation), you may *know* that you can do a job but nonetheless have difficulty convincing an interviewer to take a risk and hire you. In some cases, you can be *both* overqualified and underqualified for a role. For example, you may have more years of work experience than the role requires but not enough experience doing the *actual thing* that you would be doing.

The first step in convincing others that you can credibly shift or pivot from your "old identity" to your "new identity" is to convince *yourself.* To do that, you need to integrate (at some point, fully) the new aspects of your life into your larger world, rather than feeling like a double agent where at times you are one thing and at times another. This is harder to do when the change cannot be fully publicized (especially to your current employer) until complete, but you nonetheless need to find a way to live comfortably in your new space while still inhabiting the old.

Only if *you* are first convinced and come across as the proverbial calm, cool and collected candidate will interviewers and others buy into the change. I could give you many examples from my own life, as I have made a number of successful transitions, and they have gotten easier over time. Here are some highlights:

> *When I first graduated law school and passed the bar, I remember having a hard time calling myself an "attorney" or "lawyer" to family, friends and strangers. Fortunately, I was able to say it at the office and in front of clients without tripping up, but in social situations it felt awkward and strange. (There was only one other attorney in the family, a third cousin on my father's side. I was pummeled with questions, sideways glances and snickers about whether I liked my new job at the esteemed Dewey Cheat-Um and Howe. This had nothing to do with my new employer, of course, only how the words sounded and made the speakers feel smart for saying them.) After a few months of feeling torn, I finally realized what now seems obvious. I couldn't receive a 100% approval rating and also be true to my own choices. The jokes didn't stop, but life got much easier after that.*

> *15 years later, I became a career coach, resume writer and — for those who had known me as a lawyer — "former practicing attorney." I still get questions and the occasional disparaging remark from someone who does not understand the value of what I do or "why I would give up such a safe career," but I am completely comfortable with my choice so the comments run through me like water.*

> *Even more recently, I had an opportunity to give myself the daunting title of "author" for the very first time as I asked our local public library if they would like me to donate a copy of Master the Interview when it was published. I marveled at how easy it was to get the words out and realized that in years past it would not have been.*

The message here is that whatever you want to do, you have to *own it.* The opportunities are there for the taking, but you have to believe that they have your name on them. Once you do that, convincing others is not a matter of walking over hot coals to get where you want to be but instead simply finding a way to be of service in your new role. How can you "show up" in the right way to benefit others? If you start there, the rest falls into place.

On a very practical level, if you don't fit the call of a job exactly, below are some points to consider and convey that may put your interviewer's mind at ease that you can make a smooth transition.

Do you have examples of times that you have undertaken projects that demonstrate skills (i.e., transferable skills) that the role requires?

1) _____

_____

2) _____

_____

3) _____

_____

*Note: make sure that the above examples are responsive to the chief underlying question of any interview:* **why should I hire you?** *If you wish to demonstrate marketing skills and you are discussing a volunteer position, for example, focus on the challenges you faced and results of your efforts in the context of fundraising, maintaining donor/funder relationships and/or "selling" your organization to volunteers, beneficiaries and the public.*

How can you work the above examples into an interview? In other words, what sort of questions can you imagine that could prompt a discussion of your transferable skills?

_____

_____

What or where is the gap (i.e., what competencies are lacking, if any)? Do you need a certification or degree, or can you master these new skills on your own through classes, experience or self-learning? If you don't know, how can you find out?

_____

_____

If you do have gaps that you will need to fill in order to complete the transition and meet the expectations of your new role, what is your plan to fill them?

_____

_____

What other ways can you highlight your transferable skills?

_____

_____

_____

How can you answer a direct question about whether you are qualified for the role? (Hint: watch your eye contact and body language as you respond.)

_____

_____

_____

What do you offer that a more "traditional" job candidate might not?

_____

_____

_____

Not all job skills need to be learned in a formal setting, if you cannot devote yourself to regular or full-time study. I have a number of clients who, for example, know the basics about or outline of certain software (e.g., they took a Hadoop class in college or work with it in some capacity, but they do not know how to code in the language) and have said that they would have many more opportunities to seek out roles if they knew how to use it. My answer to that is generally two-fold: (1) if you really need to be more familiar with certain software or demonstrate a competency in problem-solving through coding generally, make a plan to learn it (and if you cannot, why not?), and (2) are you sure that is what is holding you back, or is something else making you believe that you "aren't ready" for those roles?

Regarding the second point, sometimes we find ways to limit ourselves when we are not emotionally ready for a next step, blaming it on a lack of skills so that we do not need to confront the underlying issues. Often the prerequisite to getting a job that involves coding is being a "good coder" and knowing how to "think about code," not necessarily knowing the specific language in use at a company.

MIT (yes, *that* MIT) is a great resource for online learning, as it offers free online materials, and there are others as well depending on your field and the level of competence and/or certifications that you wish to achieve. See <https://ocw.mit.edu/index.htm>. Cousera.org is another excellent online source for classes to fill gaps in your competencies, from SaaS to emotional intelligence and beyond.

## D.    You Have Taken an Extended Leave of Absence

If you are coming back to the workforce after a significant period away, I suggest that you seriously consider a "professional makeover" or "rebranding strategy" with a coach or through a formal program. How much (in terms of energy and dollars) you should invest in this process depends on the difference it will make in your self-esteem, well-being and earning power. If you decide not to go that route, consider finding someone to keep you accountable (which may be a mentor rather than another job seeker), be sure to hold a number of informational interviews in your target field and catch up with whatever developments you will need to know so that you can make up for lost time.

In addition, don't doubt yourself. You did something valuable with your time away, probably the most important thing in your life (whether raising kids, getting healthy or caring for relatives). Not every interviewer or employer will value that, but it is nonetheless valuable. Focus on the ones that see the full picture.

Finally, you may need to take a step down in order to get back to where you were before, depending on how long you have been away and how much effort you put into keeping your "hand in" the workforce. You are not alone in this process, and it is not an indicator of your worth whether you are keeping up with your peers (in terms of seniority, compensation and otherwise) who did not take leave. Regardless of your feelings about how much you can contribute and at what level, there is a "leave discount" that often attaches, which is not personal but simply a practical reality. Indicating that you are aware of this reality and willing to pay some dues upon re-entry goes a long way toward getting you back on path.

Notes: _____

## E.    You Are Pregnant

If you are pregnant and it is not obvious, you may wonder if this is information that you should (or need to) share with a future employer. In most cases, I would opt not to share. If you are reasonably concerned that your pregnancy or the first few months of the baby's life will seriously interfere with your ability to do the job – whether it requires extensive air travel or another activity or commitment you cannot meet – then you should probably discontinue the interview process and, if you have progressed to the final stages, don't take the offer. If you feel that it will not, there is no reason to "disqualify" yourself unnecessarily. I would give this advice even if you know that the company or organization is a family friendly environment. You may hit the wrong person with the news on the wrong day – maybe this person feels the policies are being abused and is concerned you will do that as well – and it can complicate your candidacy. That said, as a professional you should be honest with yourself about what the job entails and whether you will have the ability and desire to meet expectations.

If you are pregnant and it is obvious, your interviewer may nonetheless pretend not to notice, out of concerns for your privacy or to avoid asking any illegal questions. In that case,

I would address it directly, so that you have an opportunity to head off any concerns (or decide the role is not a match). Take care, however, not to let the discussion spill into a "personal chat" or otherwise derail the interview process.


Notes: _____


## F.    You Have a Visible or Hidden Disability


Disabilities can be a charged topic – even the word can raise a red flag – and many important points related to disability and employment are beyond the scope of this workbook. If you have a status or condition that qualifies as a disability, I suggest that you search for one of the many helpful resources on this topic that relate to your specific situation and consult with trusted friends or counsel. These resources can get very specific, such as the Rochester Institute of Technology's webpage on profiles in healthcare for the deaf and hard-of-hearing community. See <http://www.rit.edu/ntid/healthcare/success>. You will also find important information on the U.S. Department of Labor's Office of Disability Employment Policy website at <https://www.dol.gov/odep> and the EEOC's website (listed above in the section on "Bias and Illegal Questions" in Chapter 12).


To the extent that anyone can generalize about how to approach an interview with a disability – and the range of how disabilities affect major life activities is very broad – I would give the same advice as I have in the section above. If your disability is noticeable, it is probably a better approach to address it directly in an interview, as your interviewer will likely want to hear your "take." Otherwise, unable to discuss your disability but aware of its existence, your interviewer may be distracted and unable to give you his/her full consideration. While this does put the onus on you to address it, at the same time you have taken control of the conversation with respect to this critical part of your candidacy. In some cases, the employer may be specifically seeking out candidates who possess your specialized knowledge, insights and compassion, and if you are in a job search you can seek out which employers are poised to hire candidates with specific disabilities.


If you have a hidden disability – i.e., one not visible to the interviewer upon plain sight – you may wish to determine on your own (without disclosing it) whether the company, role and environment are a match for your physical health and will sustain your psychological health over the long term. If you choose not to disclose, I would take extra steps to ensure before accepting an offer both that you have made the right decision for yourself and that you can meet the company's needs.


Big picture questions include: Is the job a match for you? Will you thrive in the role? Will your talents and insights be (and be viewed as) an asset, so that you can grow in the role and make significant contributions?


Notes: _____

## G.     You Need or Want Part-Time or Flextime Work or Telecommuting

If you are applying to a role and will only consider part-time, flex-time and/or a work-at-home arrangement, then it behooves you to broach this topic at a convenient point in the first interview, even at the risk of disqualifying your candidacy.

As one interviewer said to me, "If I don't hear about it until the third interview, I will feel that I have been duped." What job seekers sometimes forget is that the interviewer may decline to meet with other candidates because he/she has a feeling that it will work out with the ones that are currently in the queue. If you present as a strong full-time candidate for weeks or months and only thereafter spring the news that you need to be part-time, not only will you lose credibility, but also you may not be able to meet the needs (including workload needs) of the role.

On the other hand, if you make a strong impression with an interviewer, he/she may go to bat for you, giving you a fighting chance to get the job. I know that I have done that myself, making the case that "one of her is worth two of any of the other candidates, and she can probably do the same job in half the time." Sometimes this argument succeeds, other times it fails. Still other times, the role is such that an individual needs to be available in the office, for regular hours, five days a week.

If part-time work, a flexible schedule or telecommuting is not a requirement but rather a hope or strong request, you may decide at what point to ask if either is a possibility depending on your best appraisal of the employer as well as your timeframe to find a new opportunity.

Notes: _____

## H.     You Have a Questionable Element in Your Background

If your background includes a criminal conviction or other serious point that needs to be overcome, you may want to seek out a career coach to help position you for your next role and know how to discuss what happened, what you have learned and how you have moved on and are ready for the role. Generally, you should be upfront and honest without offering unnecessary details.

At the same time, you should consider whether a change of field or job responsibilities is needed. For example, if you were barred from the securities industry due to a misrepresentation or trading on insider information, you may find it difficult to get any job that allows you discretion with funds (i.e., other people's money) or highly confidential documents, whether or not your settlement allows reentry into the industry or the position is outside of financial services. Each individual case is different, and you should carefully consider what options are realistic for you and how to pursue them.

A questionable element in your candidacy may arise for many reasons, however, and they are not all a result of your own actions or errors. You may have an ex-spouse who filed for bankruptcy, your prior firm may have gone under or been investigated, your former partners may have been indicted for fraud or you may have even made the national news for "kidnapping" your children to get out of reach of an abusive spouse.

Some of these events may have happened after you left a firm (or after your divorce) and/or be entirely unrelated to you (or misconstrued), nonetheless they arise in a Google search or background check, or they may otherwise be better disclosed upfront. There are often ways to position your personal brand to distance yourself from these unfortunate events or otherwise explain them, while being honest, as the truth always comes out. (You would rather, I assume, pass on a job than take it and find yourself in an inhospitable environment or out of work, once discovered.) Again, if any of these situations applies to you, I would suggest you speak with a professional versed in this area who can help you frame the circumstances and put up your best forward in your career documents and the interview process.

Notes: _____

## I.    You Are an International Candidate

If you are an international candidate, there are a number of specific concerns that may be applicable to your candidacy, including whether you will need visa sponsorship, be a cultural fit and/or have language barriers that make communication difficult. It behooves you as a candidate to think through these issues from the perspective of the employer and do what you can to troubleshoot or bridge any gaps. Sometimes you will be hired on the basis of your work product alone, at least in some fields. In other cases, you may need to work harder to present yourself as a preferred candidate or consider taking a bridge job (i.e., a short term role that is not your first choice) in order to make the transition happen on a timely basis.

Notes: _____

## J.    Other Special Considerations

Hopefully the principles above have helped you discern how to approach any additional circumstances that you may face which require special consideration during the interview process. If not, you may wish to seek out a book or article devoted to the specific topic or work with a career coach to get your answers.

Final Notes:

_____

_____

# CHAPTER 15
# BEHIND THE SCENES
# (THE INTERVIEWER'S SIDE)

*There's nothing worse than being nervous for an interview when you're the interviewer.*
-Business Owner

*I would rather not hire anyone than hire the wrong person.*
– Financial Services Executive

If you have never interviewed someone (i.e., sat on the hiring side of the table), then it may be difficult to imagine what it looks like – and what *you* look like – from that perspective. Yet it is critically important to do so, since the interviewer's perspective informs all of your actions as an interviewee.

We all say we want to be better at interviewing, but only those who can see their interview presentation through the interviewer's eyes will actually learn how to sail through them (or, failing that, get the job). Case in point: I cannot tell you how many times I have given interviewing advice, and as I am in the middle of delivering a helpful feedback of how someone is not coming across as intended, the person is shaking his or her "yes" but I don't see the proverbial light bulbs going on in their heads. In other words, I know that the comment was not internalized, and there will be no change in behavior. It is like the actor who keeps expressing fear rather than surprise. He will not be in many more shows, neither for that director nor (likely) any other.

Notes: _____

You need to light the light bulb and keep it lit during the interview. If you turn back to the Introduction of this workbook, I offered some common critiques that I have given to clients. You can start there, and see if any of those apply to you. You can also recall and write down any critiques that you have received from former interviewers, in mock interviews and from friends. You are identifying these mistakes not to dwell on them, but so you can learn from them and master the craft of interviewing, which will take you quite far in life.

> *Be sensitive to the reactions of the interviewer; if what you are saying bores him, choose something else [to discuss].*
> – Michael Shurtleff, Audition

If I haven't mentioned it already, above all never bore your interviewer. Watch how your words are being received. If you have lost your interviewer's attention, it doesn't matter how important (you believe) the point is that you are making. You will fall flat, because the interviewer doesn't care. In the interview, you have an audience of one (or small group, if a panel). Make every word count.

Imagine for a moment that you are an actor rehearsing on stage. In response to a fellow actor's line, which you have heard at least twenty times already in prior rehearsals, the script calls for you to express surprise. You lift your hands up into the air, drop open your jaw and make your best "surprised" face. Now imagine the director is in the orchestra pit calling out, "Lift your hands higher! They can't see your expression that way. You need to do more!" Or saying, "That doesn't come across as surprise. It looks more like fear from here. Can you try it again?" What would your response be? Would you try harder to express surprise, find it somewhere inside of you and ramp it up until it worked, or would you shrug and think "to hell with the audience if they didn't get it"? The best actors, of course, find a way to go deeper and connect further, even on their worst days. That is why we love them. We feel right along with them, we go where they lead, because we are enthralled by their portrayal of the experience.

*Have you ever enthralled someone in an interview? Have you even thought that possible? What if you were exactly the candidate that the interviewer was looking for and you excelled at every interview test thrown at you? Is that result worthy of your time and aspiration?*

I am not the first person to compare interviewing to acting, and I certainly won't be the last. It is fundamentally different, of course, because you are working to be yourself, not someone else. Yet you still have a part to play – the best version of yourself, and the one who fits the bill for the job – rather than simply showing up and having a conversation.

Notes: _____

## A.   The Hiring Decision

I have served on multiple teams of interviewers in various contexts, and at the end of the day the hiring decision was often reduced to the same short list of criteria, whether or not we used these words or formulated them as concrete questions:

*Did we each believe this person could do the job?* (question of competence)

*Is this person the best fit for the job from the pool of applicants in front of us, or should we consider extending the interviews?* (question of fit)

*Was he/she excited about working for us?* (question of fit)

*Will she/he work hard?* (question of dedication)

*Will she/he be a good individual contributor and also work well as a team?* (question of fit)

*Do I trust him/her? Were his/her answers consistent among the interviews?* (questions of credibility)

*Did we really like him/her? Would we want to work with him/her day in and day out? Would others?* (questions of likeability)

*Will he/she be happy here and in this role (or, in some contexts, happy enough)?* (question of fit)

*Will he/she accept the compensation we are offering and stay here for at least a few years without looking to "trade up"?* (questions of longevity and "financial fit")

Did you notice that most of the questions boiled down to fit? As one interviewer said to me, "If the candidate has the right personality and seems generally competent, he/she can usually learn whatever specific skills we need."

Notes: _____

## B.    Interviewer Personalities

Whether you know your INTJs from your ESFPs (i.e., the letters that help define personality types under the Meyers-Briggs Type Indicator®), you can appreciate and likely recognize that interviewers have different traits and styles that contribute to how they conduct an interview and whether they will respond well to different approaches you may adopt to the interview format or types of responses you may give. Lou Adler teaches in his book *Hire with Your Head* that there are three basic interviewer styles: emotional, intuitive or technical. Susan Whitcomb, whose certified career management coach training I completed when I first became a coach, adds a fourth style: the performance-based interviewer. These styles essentially break down as follows:

- *Technical interviewer* – technical interviewers focus on whether you have the technical skills for the job, sometimes to the exclusion of whether you can actually use them properly. If you have a technical interviewer, make sure to be logical and sequential in your responses. In addition, if the interviewer is quizzing you on skills you lack, follow up with a straightforward example of a time that you used a similar skill set.

- *Emotional interviewer* – emotional interviewers base their perceptions on whether they "click" with you in the interview, and first impressions are extremely important. Be thoughtful in your responses, and watch for any disconnect in the discussion or indication of a less than positive reaction. If you sense that the interview is moving away from you, it may be time for a more direct approach: "May I give you some examples of what I envision for this role?"

- *Intuitive interviewer* – intuitive interviewers tend to make decisions based on gut reactions. If they believe a candidate is capable in a few critical areas, they will believe that he/she can do anything asked. As a result, they may not get the critical information they need to "sell" your candidacy to the other decision-makers, because in their mind you are already qualified. You can help make the sale to the other key stakeholders by stressing your mastery and progress in key areas.

- *Performance-based interviewer* – performance-based interviewers focus on competencies, so you should emphasize your skills and your ability to be practical, innovative and effective.

Adler further notes that interviewers tend to hire "in their same image," which does not necessarily mean they look for similar race, gender, academics or other traits, although it certainly can. For example, logic-driven executives have a tendency to hire these same candidates, while creative managers tend to hire candidates more like them. If you are a candidate who is very different from the interviewer, try to be aware of their biases and bridge the gap by presenting common ground or demonstrating how your differences present you an advantage. ("You seem to be a big picture person. I can understand why you need someone to take care of the details.") Interviewers who have become aware of their tendencies and seek to correct them may not squarely fit into any of the discrete categories above but may have learned (through training or discussions with colleagues) how to use diverse criteria and approaches to evaluate a candidate rather than relying on a single point of view.

Notes:  _____

## C.    Company and Departmental Personalities

In addition to being aware of the personality of your interviewer, also consider the "personality" of the company (and individual department) with which you are interviewing. As Christopher Wein, Tax Performance Advisory Manager at Ernst & Young, said:

> *"The type of company with which you are interviewing makes a tremendous difference in how you should approach the process. At our firm, for example, we are very focused on someone's ability to set and meet goals. We may ask you in an interview how you set up your to-do-list for the day or week and how much of it you accomplish. In other contexts, such as a law firm, they will have other priorities. At the same time, as you go through many levels of interviews, you should take a different approach to each one, tailored to the seniority, orientation and individual needs of the person with whom you are meeting."*

## D.    Teams of Interviewers

When I work with job candidates to prepare them for interviews, I try to drive home the point that there are many things going on behind the scenes about which they may never be aware. It may even be that an interviewer who seems distant and non-responsive is like the proverbial duck – smooth on the surface but furiously paddling underneath – and working to be the candidate's best advocate among a diversity of goals and viewpoints on the interviewing team.

As one interviewer shared with me, you cannot always account for how members of your team will act in an interview. Some may be very good at interviewing candidates, while others may come across as threatening, awkward, self-absorbed, non-committal or otherwise. As a member of an interviewing team, you have to find a way to work with the players that you have.

To some degree, it is important as a candidate to drill down and figure out what is "really going on" in the dynamics of the interviewing team and firm. At the same time, you don't want overanalyze every single step of the process. If an interviewer seems awkward, maybe he/she is. The important question is to what extent you'll be working with that individual, and whether the awkwardness or other trait seems like it will interfere with (or not provide support for) a positive working environment.

Notes:  _____

## E.      What Else is Going On?

One last point I should mention about the "interviewer's perspective" is that there is often more going on behind the scenes than the employer is willing or able to communicate. At times, there has been some drama or upheaval that lead to an open position, or there are other factors playing into the company's decisions and interview process. You may pick up some undertones through insightful questions, and close attention to the delivery of the answers, such as, "Is this a newly created role?" or "How would I interact with the rest of the team?"

While I wouldn't pry or try to force an interviewer to spill the beans, which may make you seem pushy, I would ask *around* the issue to try to see what you can uncover. If you are told that someone resigned and get an odd feeling about the interviewer's tone, you may ask in an upbeat voice, "Oh, where did he/she end up next?" or "I'll bet that was disappointing. How long was he/she here?"

Candidates and interviewers have shared a range of situations with me about these so-called hidden factors that go into hiring. One candidate, for example, said that she was told the candidate had resigned but, months later, was still unemployed. "In retrospect, that probably should have been a red flag for me to follow up through the grapevine, about whether this person left because the job was just so damn frustrating," she said.

Employers, on the other hand, may have done everything right but nonetheless ended up in a tough spot with hope that they can still present a seamless hiring experience to potential candidates. As Laurie Davis Edwards, Founder and CEO of eFlirt, recounted that she extended an offer to a second choice candidate for a key position at the firm after her first choice accepted and then not only failed to show up for work the first day but also to communicate why or what had happened. She told me:

> *"I was worried she may have been in an accident and even wondered if I should report her missing. I frankly had no idea what to do. We were so excited for her to start working for us, and then she was suddenly MIA.*
>
> *On what would have been her third day at work, this employee (in name only) finally got back in touch, professing immigration issues and other reasons which clearly did not go far enough in explaining why she couldn't have placed a phone call or sent an email.*
>
> *To make matters worse, I was on a major client pitch during the entire situation – addressing all of this remotely – trying to stay "on" for my meetings while feeling completely out of sorts about whether we should continue to follow up or cut our losses.*

*I finally called Candidate #2 to extend the offer, after confirmation from our attorney that we could essentially "fire" the first candidate with no ramifications (after sending warning and termination notices, that were each returned to sender). I was nervous about whether our other candidate – whom I was also excited about hiring – would accept, wondering if there would ever be a moment in the future that I could tell her the full story. Thankfully, this second person said yes immediately, joined us shortly thereafter and has been a great fit ever since."*

# CHAPTER 16
# AFTER THE INTERVIEW

### A.      Take Time to Debrief

If you have ever worked with a recruiter, you will notice that recruiters invariably request a debriefing shortly after your interview. I always valued these calls rather highly, because it was helpful to hear the recruiter's perspective and have a chance to "hear myself talk" about the opportunity. At the same time, I knew that I needed to have room to think in my own quiet space, without any external influences.

If your first step after your interview is talking to a recruiter (or anyone else, such as a spouse or parent), also make notes for yourself while the meetings are fresh in your mind. Sometimes we lose our train of thought once new information enters the picture, such as questions from others or re-entry into the mix of a current job situation.

If you do not have time to make written notes within the first few hours after the interview but do have the opportunity to record yourself (e.g., in a recording app on your phone), I highly suggest you do the latter and transcribe your notes, or at least email the recording to yourself for safekeeping. You will want to have these notes in front of you when you return for additional interviews and while evaluating (if applicable) multiple offers, and you may even want to keep them for future job searches.

Points to include in your debrief are:

1.      Your Overall Impressions
2.      Thoughts About the Interviewer and Company
3.      Points About You to Emphasize in Future Interviews
4.      Points About the Employer or Role to Emphasize in Future Interviews
5.      Any "Bottom Line" or Potential Stocking Points on Compensation, etc.
6.      Further Questions to Have Answered
7.      Further People to Meet
8.      Pros and Cons vs. Other Potential Roles
9.      Areas of Improvement for Future Interviews
10.    Additional Thoughts or Concerns

I have included a worksheet on the following two pages, which you can copy and use for multiple interviews. You can also access additional worksheets at www.annemariesegal.com. (Click on "Worksheets.")

## <u>Post-Interview Debrief Form</u>

**Company:** _____

**Date:** _____

**Stage/Type of Interview:** _____

Overall Impressions

_____

_____

_____

Thoughts About the Interviewer or Company

_____

_____

_____

Points About <u>Me</u> to Emphasize in Future Interviews

_____

_____

_____

Points About the Employer or Role to Emphasize in Future Interviews

_____

_____

_____

Any "Bottom Line" or Potential Sticking Points on Compensation, etc.

_____

_____

_____

Further Questions to Have Answered

_____

_____

_____

Further People to Meet

_____

_____

Pros and Cons vs. Other Potential Roles

_____

_____

_____

Areas of Improvement for Future Interviews

_____

_____

_____

_____

**B.**     **Thank-You Notes**

In virtually all circumstances, you should send a personalized thank-you note to each interviewer within 24 hours of the interview. (If your interview is on a Friday, you can follow up during the weekend or on the next business day.) There is a distinct art to the thank-you note, namely that you should keep the tone light and optimistic, reference relevant points that arose in your conversation, note again how you will add value to the team and (if needed) diplomatically dispel any concerns that may have arise during the interview process.

The hardest part of a thank-you note is often getting started:

> *I appreciate you speaking with me yesterday about the opportunities [in the _____ department] of [Name of Company]. It was a pleasure to learn more about you and your team, especially the [_____] project….*

While some interviewers value handwritten notes, email has become the standard way to communicate in this context, as it is quick, efficient and virtually guaranteed to be received by the intended recipient. (Clearly, if you know your interviewer does not like or use email, then send your thank-you message by regular mail.)

If you have not received the email address of an interviewer before or during the interview, and you do not have an easy way to obtain it, you can either send an email to your direct contact (such as a third-party or in-house recruiter) for forwarding to the interviewer or write a group email to one individual and thank all interviewers in the same message. In some companies, due to productivity concerns, the in-house recruiting teams do not want to encourage job seekers to have continued contact with their employees unless and until the employees reach out directly, so the forwarded email will allow you to show diligent follow-up nonetheless. Alternatively, you can send a hand-written note (and you may choose to do that as well, as an extra effort), but as I mentioned above, this can take a few days to post, so if the interview process is brisk, it may not be timely.

I suggest you write a polite thank-you note even if you never intend to work for the company. You never know whether you may change your mind, circumstances may change or the same individuals may be good contacts at a prior date (whether at that company or following a transition of their own).

Most importantly, keep your thank-you note clear and to the point. The thank-you note is again an opportunity to answer that same question (which by now may sound redundant, but is nonetheless true): *why should we hire you?*

If you want to go above and beyond in the thank-you note in an attempt to "seal the deal," one way to impress an employer is to write out your 30-60-90 day action plan for the new role (i.e., your vision of how you will tackle the problems that an employer has presented in the interview, prioritizing them into the first 30, 60 and 90 days, or even six months, on the job). As Rebecca Bosl, Founder and CEO of the Dream Life Team, LLC, has said:

> *"In the interview, ask what a successful candidate should accomplish in the first 90 days, and use this intelligence to send a 90-day action plan to the employer within the first 24 hours after the interview. The hiring manager will receive your action plan at about the same time he or she receives the other thank-you notes. This will help you to stand out – you'll look brilliant and miles ahead of everyone else."*

Of course, writing out a plan for how you would solve problems for the employer is a considerable investment of time, and it only makes sense for roles in which you can "take the reins" and get things done. Yet the investment of time that you make at the outset – not only to make a good impression but also to think through the relevant issues and show how you will tackle them – is why this approach is so effective. Only a candidate who is serious about the role and willing to make the effort to demonstrate that will take this extra step.

## C.    The Waiting Game

> *"Everyone tells you what they think you want to hear. They say they have an expedited schedule and then never call you back."*
> - Mid-Level Job Candidate

It is easy to get discouraged if you are excited about a company and then have weeks of so-called "radio silence" after the interview or a string of delays in scheduling a callback.

The worst part about interviewing may not be the interview itself. It may be the time period after the interview, which can last anywhere from a day (lucky you) to a year (or longer, if the company enters into an extended hiring freeze or is restructuring). Generally the longest wait is a few months, and you may be right many times, but not always, to conclude that a company that cannot finalize the selection process is overly bureaucratic or disorganized. Sometimes the delay is due to other factors, such as difficulty coordinating meeting times among candidates and multiple interviewers or vacation and travel schedules of individuals who need to be part of the interview or approval process or a company "emergency" that has taken precedence. When interviewing on behalf of employers, I was always surprised with the job seekers who acted as if their candidacy was *the priority* for the entire department or company. Very likely, it is not. In addition, the more senior the candidate, the more cautious and calculated the company will be.

*Sometimes, however, you do not hear back at all, even if they sounded like they loved you. In those cases, you may feel bewildered and will not have closure, but you still need to move on.*

During the waiting period, you will want to continue to follow up and express on-going interest (rather than nag). Depending on the circumstances, phone calls or email may be more appropriate, so I do not want to give any hard and fast rules here. If you are in doubt, follow up by email to the company or recruiter, as applicable, unless your job would require you to "close sales," in which case you may prefer to make contact by phone to show you have what it takes to get the sale done.

The key is not to become a pest. If you call multiple times and the interviewer is not available, you may consider saying that "you will call back" rather than leave a message. Alternatively, you can leave a complete voicemail with the reason you are calling and your contact information, and then wait again for a return call or email. Sound upbeat, as though you are the top candidate, whether or not you believe it. The worst thing is to sound nervous or dejected, even if you feel those emotions at any point. Another suggestion from a frequent interviewer is to follow up with the company with further questions or input about your candidacy, which is a no-pressure way to engage them and express ongoing interest.

If you continue to interview with other companies while waiting for a response – which I highly suggest you do – you may receive an offer from a second company while waiting to hear from the first. In that case, you can go back to the first company (if it is the employer you would prefer), note that you remain highly interested in working for them and that you have another offer outstanding. This may prompt them to make a decision more quickly. While I would not give the company a deadline to respond, which sounds presumptuous, you should let them know your deadline to accept or reject the other offer. For this tactic to be effective, you need to let the first company know as soon as you can, so they have as much time as possible to coordinate, decide and make an offer.

## D.   Continued Follow Up (Without Being a Pain)

In the early weeks following your interview, I would generally follow up every two weeks if you have not heard back from the company. As time progresses, this may move to every three weeks, and beyond a few months from your last interview you may wish to keep in contact every month or two. Of course, this differs depending on the circumstances, so I suggest it only as a guide. Polite, consistent follow-up is important, as it keeps you top of mind while others may fade into the distance.

## E.   Evaluating an Opportunity

There is a wealth of information – and considerable misinformation – about large public companies and often very little on private ones. As a result, it can often be difficult to decipher the culture into which you are heading. In fact, one of the largest sources of workplace dissatisfaction is that a job candidate expected he/she was making certain tradeoffs, the obvious one being less pay for better quality of life, only to find out that there was no trade: the job is worse than other alternatives in both respects.

*Know Your Priorities and Consider the Tradeoffs*

What makes a good place for you to work? This differs among candidates and depends on what they are hoping to achieve in a particular role and their career generally.

For example, when speaking with junior attorneys I have often referred to the formative process (if done right) in their early years as an extended form of boot camp. There is such a high level of substantive knowledge and judgment that needs to be acquired in a short time in order to succeed in one's career. This same need to start one's career with a sustained intensity is present in other fields, medicine being a notable and obvious one.

The value in such case is that one will build and possess a solid set of skills and, hopefully, reputation to match. People who are drawn to such careers may also value intellectual challenge, stimulating colleagues and, in some cases, high compensation. To achieve these ends, they may accept tradeoffs such as lack of time for, commitment to or flexibility in their personal lives or even lack of sleep. At the same time, they should be aware of possible hidden tradeoffs in some cases such as lack of mentoring, insular work environments and little control over career direction, which differ by employer, role and individual. You can think of these as "downsides" and "upsides," and the point is not to make a general value judgment about them but to decide for yourself what are your priorities at each stage of your career.

This is simply one example, and there is clearly a whole range of tradeoffs to consider, from where you will need to live if you take the role to how stable the company appears to be.

If you have not yet examined your values, it may be that you are simply doing "what everyone else does" and not necessarily asking yourself if a job offer makes sense for you. Over time, if we do not choose our values, they are chosen for us.

*Do Your Homework*

Doing proper due diligence on a company involves a mix of official, authoritative and unofficial sources, as well as individual discussions with employees, if you are able to make a connection with someone you trust. Remember that if a company has many departments or offices, the working environment can vary tremendously from one area to another.

So where do you get your information? If you are interviewing at Google, for example, you could read William Poundstone's book, *Are You Smart Enough to Work at Google?* Don't take at face value, however, that his discussions of Google perks are an accurate representation of the *environment that you will enter* at the time that you are entering into it. He wrote:

> *"The quintessential Google perk isn't sashimi or massages. It's the 20 percent project. Google engineers are allowed to spend one day a week on a project of their choosing. That's a fantastic gamble…. At Google, it works. It's been reported that over half of Google's revenue now comes from ideas that began as 20 percent time projects. The list includes Gmail, Google Maps, Google News, Google Sky, and Google Voice."*

You can easily find (through a *Google* search, irony noted) insiders who are quick to discredit the claim that Google is a haven of meaningful work that changes the world or that "20 percent" time even exists in practical terms. One highly popular user thread on Quora.com, for example, stated that:

*"[E]very Googler that joined after mid 2000s and is below L8, knows that 20% does not exist, but somehow, [the] media keeps making it sound like it actually exists. For most of the Googlers, 20% is really what you do outside of your 100% time…."*

Note: To read the thread, please visit <https://www.quora.com/What-are-the-negatives-in-working-in-a-too-good-to-be-true-offices-like Google/answers/13959582/share>.

As a job seeker, which sources do you believe or, more specifically, how much weight do you put on each one? Whether it is a published book, a reputable website or an aggregator of comments from named and anonymous sources, you have to decide what you believe and hope that your estimation is correct.

Here's my take on it: don't assume that any answer is black-and-white but allow that there may be some gray. Your goal is to determine if it is a darker gray or a lighter gray (e.g., if the comments you are hearing tend to put the company in a favorable or unfavorable light).

In other words, how much should you discount or trust each piece of information in making your decision? The more data points you have, the better you can make the right call. In any case, if a certain representation about a company is a critical part of your decision, and that representation has been discounted or discredited, then you need to dig deep to find the "truth" before accepting the offer. In some cases, you will not be able to get comfortable with how a company really operates. In others, you may need to ask a question point blank and judge whether you can trust the response. While most employers – not all – do not lie, there are some for whom hope springs eternal, and they will feel justified telling you what you want to hear. Listen to your gut and make your best decision, knowing that if you are still unsure and accept an offer, you may want to start working rather promptly on one or more contingency plans.

So check the Glassdoor reviews and any other online information, check with prior contacts (and try to find a neutral source on the inside, if you don't know anyone), read the company's site and press (if any), and assemble a mosaic of information to do the best you can to get an accurate representation of the company, your group and the role.

*Conduct In-Person Diligence*

Even if you have researched a potential employer extensively during the interview process, you may need to follow up further after the interview to get the "real scoop." Usually the best way to do this is to go right to the source: the employees with whom you will be working.

If an opportunity is presented ask further questions about the target employer after receiving an offer, I would definitely take it, even if you are very busy at your old company (and life) and feel that you cannot invest the time or that you already have a strong feeling about your decision. If no such opportunity is offered, I would try to create one. What you learn can be extremely insightful, not only to confirm your decision but also to help you adjust to the new company and be ready to troubleshoot any concerns if and when you arrive.

Most importantly, I would try to connect with people at your same level outside of the office, if they are willing to meet you for drinks, lunch or coffee. Just the act of meeting them away from the employer's location will put them at ease and indicate that you are seeking an informal, honest conversation. Failing that, you can ask to meet at their office but try to make sure (without belaboring the point) that the door is closed, or meet in a quiet conference room away from the "action" of the day.

When you hold or attend these follow-up meetings, I would not ask anyone to spill all the stories or indicate in any way that you are on the fence about joining, just say that as a matter of course you always seek more data points to be more informed about your decisions. You can follow up with open questions designed to elicit telling responses, "so can you tell me more about Tom?" (to know more about your future boss) or "have you taken any two week vacations since you've been there, or is it usually a week at a time?" (to gain insight about how the vacation policy actually works and whether people take vacation).

You may not hear all of the answers you are looking for, with an especially conservative or introverted employee – and that is helpful information for you as well, that someone you will be working with is a "vault" who rarely opens up – but often asking open-ended questions will signal the responses that you are looking for. Remember that the goal is not to ferret out *all* information but to target the information that you need to make the right decision.

*Get Your "Ducks in a Row"*

If you are between careers or undecided about your future, don't jump at the first opportunity that presents itself, but don't put your head in the sand either. Spend focused time thinking not only about a present opportunity but how it will shape your career for the long-term. Sometimes a job functions as a stepping-stone, also called a "bridge job." The chief question in that case may where the bridge will lead and how quickly you can cross it.

On another note, if you have been planning a career transition – whether it is simply a new job or an entirely new career – and your tummy feels funny when the offer comes through, listen to that voice. Your gut is pretty smart. What is it trying to tell you? Is the role wrong for you, or are you simply fearful about what else in your life needs to change to make your dream a reality? Is it time to walk the path?

*Know What You're Worth and Your Bottom Line*

There are resources that can give you ranges for salaries in certain roles, but compensation can vary widely. Recruiters are also helpful sources for this information as well as market contacts you develop over time. Sometimes, however, the most important number is the one that motivates you to move, so ask yourself what that number would be. One of my clients, for example, decided that he would need to be paid 15% more overall (all other things about the job being equal) to make a move worth his while. Otherwise, he was going to stay put.

Here are some salary resources to consider:

Department of Labor information: <www.bls.gov/oco>

The Riley Guide: <www.rileyguide.com/salary.html>

Salary.com: <www.salary.com>

Federal government jobs: <https://www.opm.gov>

You can also check with professional associations of which you are a member or go to job search sites, such as Indeed, Monster or Career Builder, or conduct a Google search with "salary" and the name of the site.

*Consider Other Factors*

As you are evaluating opportunities, don't forget to consider factors that relate to the company or industry as a whole, not only your role. For example, what is the financial health of the company? Is it growing? How strong is the management, and has there been any internal strife or bad press? If it is in a turnaround, what is the likelihood it will succeed, and could its problems create issues for you at a later stage in your career? Alternatively, could the turmoil be the exact combination needed to create a great opportunity for you?

## F.      Negotiations

Any time that you do not simply agree to the terms first presented in a job offer, you have a negotiation process to navigate. Negotiations are not present in every career transition, but they are in many, especially for more senior candidates and/or entrepreneurial roles. The question of whether you should negotiate an offer is an intricate one, and often it depends on how close the original offer is to your personal bottom line, how much you want or need a new role (i.e., how much you are willing to risk that your negotiations fail) and what you think the market (and individual employer) will bear.

Some negotiations are very delicate and best done with the help of a solution-oriented employment lawyer, coach and/or personal "board of advisors" who know your industry and can help you think through your points and how to approach the negotiation process. (Note: If you are working with a recruiter, he/she should be on that team but not your only sounding board.) Given the possible stress of negotiations, especially ones that go into multiple rounds, you want to stay calm and clear-headed. For example, if your proposed new terms are not received well by the employer, or seem to have been ignored in a revised draft of your employment agreement, you will need to determine how to react. Often, the best policy is to come to these discussions from a place of curiosity: "Is it possible you missed my comment on Section 6(a) or am I misunderstanding why you didn't accept that change?" Don't overdo it, of course. If there are many terms that you asked for that were not accepted, you may be getting the signal that they are not open to negotiating.

On the other hand, sometimes you can sound too agreeable during negotiations, e.g., due to a wish to close the deal and get started working, in which case you may agree to a set of employment terms that you would not (before receiving the offer) have imagined that you would accept. If your change of heart is due to some other great feature of the job – like a better location but a lower salary – then it may make sense to agree to such terms.

Alternatively, if you are returning from a long leave or period of unemployment, or changing fields, in some cases you will need to accept a lower compensation package than you would have wished. Make sure, however, that you are not agreeing to unacceptable terms simply because of the fear that if you don't, you will never find other suitable employment. Starting out with sour grapes about your employment package generally doesn't end well, because you simply build up resentment over time.

If you decide to negotiate, you first need to figure out what points are your priorities and whether your strategy is to ask for everything that you "would like to have" knowing that you may not get everything or ask for only those key points that you "must have" in order to take the offer. Lawyers sometimes call these must-have points ones that you will "go to the mat" on. Using the same lingo, you cannot go to the mat on every point but must determine those that matter most to you, so that you do not over-negotiate and give the impression that you are a disagreeable or difficult candidate.

If you choose to keep your negotiating points to only a few must-have issues, it may make sense to communicate that the points you have raised will be decisive in whether you will accept the offer. (For example: "I am very interested in this role, but it only makes sense for me if we can agree to the following points: [then list your points in a clear and concise format, such as bullet points].")

At other times, you may not have any points that are deal-breakers but nonetheless wish to negotiate to "see what you can get." Some job seekers decide that they will always negotiate in this manner, because they feel they have nothing to lose. (This is often, but not always, correct.) As an employer, I may say that I will pay you $140,000 a year, and you ask for $160,000. That risk can be worth taking as long as there is not a line of other qualified and desirable candidates who are very happy to work for $140,000 or even $135,000. There are ways to ask the question, of course, to facilitate a discussion. "I am really interested in this position, but the salary is not what I expected. My proposed range was $140,000 to $160,000. Can we get it move it up at all? How about $150,000?" This way, you haven't given a bottom line, but you are negotiating nonetheless.

If you are negotiating complex points or feel that you will need to be cautious about how you ask for certain revisions to the employment offer, you may wish to ask for an in-person meeting rather than work by email or phone (as is sometimes more common). Meeting face-to-face allows you to observe body language and possibly tailor your responses to curtail (or increase) what you are requesting accordingly. Make sure whenever possible that whoever is representing the employer in the negotiations is actually empowered to come to an agreement with you. If there are multiple parties that need to be involved – and you are valuable enough that they will devote time to doing it – you may wish to ask to have everyone in a room together. This is particularly important if different people at your new employer have an appreciation for different points that you wish to negotiate but none has an appreciation for all of the points.

If you have completed various negotiations in the past – whether for jobs or in other contexts – you will know that each one of them can have a "breaking point." This is the point at which the other party says, "Forget it. This is not worth the trouble." Make sure not to push past that point, because you will find that the door swings closed, and it is very likely that you will not be able to revive the discussions. Of course, you never know *exactly* where that point will be until you are almost upon it, but you can often tell from how the language (or body language) of the other person in the negotiations changes. If you are not good at reading other people for how far you can push something without blowing your objective, ask a five-year-old for advice. (Honestly!)

Another critical point to remember with negotiations is that they are not over when the deal is agreed in concept: *always get it in writing.* If you are promised something that is a key feature in your willingness to accept an offer, it needs to be documented (and should also be signed, if at all possible). For example, you may ask that since you cannot be paid a pro-rated, year-end bonus, your compensation or bonus be increased the following year. By the time that date arrives for your raise or second year bonus, the person who hired you may no longer be with the firm, or he/she may conveniently "forget" the conversation. Unfortunately, it happens all the time. Get your deal reduced to writing, or take the risk that what you think you have been promised is not what you will actually receive.

*This point – "always get it in writing" – applies to the job offer generally. In almost all cases, you should not accept a new role until you have received the written offer and any related paperwork. This means that you should not quit your old job – as much as you may want to do that – until both you and the employer have signed on the dotted line.*

Also, check what conditions there are, if any, on your offer. Conditions are essentially ways that the employer can wiggle out of making good on the offer, from background checks and drug testing to references. If possible, ask that your references are checked before your offer letter is issued (or finalized), so that you can delete this as a condition to employment. (Drug testing, on the other hand, generally is not done until after the offer letter is signed.)

Conservatively, unless there is a timing issue with your old firm that behooves you to share sooner, I would not give notice at a prior role until you have a countersigned offer letter and all of the conditions to the offer have been met. I also would not cancel any other interviews that you may have pending, even if you no longer actively pursue the job search.

## G.     Employee Handbooks, Policies and Benefits

Prior to accepting an offer, you should ask for, receive and review the company's employee handbook, compliance manual (if any) and other policies and procedures applicable to you.

Often these documents and any agreements you must sign are referenced in an offer letter, and you can follow up asking for copies of each document referenced.

If a company resists supplying its handbook or policies for any reason other than a concern that it is "too soon" in the process – and you will need to evaluate if that is true – I would not accept an offer. Ethical, fair companies are above-board and open about their policies, and if they are not, it should raise some serious red flags. On the other hand, very small companies or and smaller non-profit institutions may not have full-blown handbooks, although you should nonetheless be provided any policies to which you will be subject. If they have no written policies, depending on the nature of the role, that may be a cause for concern.

Employee handbooks generally follow a certain pattern and cover everything from basic benefits and vacation/leave to employee expectations, and the range of topics is too broad to cover all details here. For example, they also may include, by virtue of your signature, consent to ongoing background checks and recording of your phone conversations on company lines.

If, for any reason, you need to request an exception to the handbook or a representation you have been asked to make, this should be carefully documented. Note that not all companies will grant these exceptions, and you should ask sparingly so you do not arouse suspicions about why you cannot agree to their standard terms.

Some companies have instituted delays for participation in 401(k) plans and, in some cases, health plans. Be sure to ready everything carefully and make sure you understand it before signing.

## H.    Noncompetition and Related Agreements

Before accepting an offer, you should also confirm whether there is a noncompetition ("noncompete") or related agreement. If there is one, do not feel compelled to sign it without sufficient time to review. They can apply in many contexts, even if you are not a high-level employee. My former beautician, for example, mentioned that at a salon at which she interviewed required all employees to sign a noncompete as a condition to employment. It would have prohibited her, if she had signed it, from launching her own salon within a 50-mile radius of the employer. (Note: while not all provisions are enforceable, in some cases the real issue may not be one of enforceability but of the time and expense of hiring a lawyer and going to court to defend your rights.)

Noncompete agreements can become highly complex very quickly, so a short overview is not sufficient to address every important point (nor is this legal advice). That said, here are some of the points you should consider:

1) **Do you understand the plain language of the contract you are signing?** If not, have it reviewed by someone who does and who understands how the laws work in the jurisdiction governing the agreement. This person does not need to be a lawyer, but in some cases really should be. The greater your obligations and risk of them interfering with any future employment, the more likely an attorney review is appropriate. At the same time, do not assume that all attorneys, by virtue of passing the bar, understand noncompetition provisions.

2) **If the agreement prohibits you from taking other employment for a certain time period, are you compensated for taking on that obligation?** This could apply if you resign or are fired. In the latter case, severance provisions may be included in the contract.

3) **Is the agreement actually a "noncompetition" agreement, or is it only a "nonsolicitation" agreement?** If you are not used to reading these provisions, everything can begin to sound alike. A "noncompete" means you will not compete. A "nonsolicit" (sometimes colloquially called a "non-poach") means you will not hire, interfere with, steal away, etc., some group of individuals associated with the company in some way, whether they are employees, customers or others.

   Note that sometimes there are parties included in a nonsolicitation clause who may not be appropriate in your particular case, such as "potential clients" (however defined). In fact, coming to agreement on what language properly circumscribes the group is often a key value that attorney representation adds. You do not want to save a few thousand dollars on a contract review and lose out on hundreds of thousands (or even millions) because you later cannot do what you thought you could.

4) **Note that noncompete clauses can be embedded in other documents.** For example, a shareholders agreement (if you will become a shareholder of the firm) may include noncompetition language.

5) **Noncompetition and/or nonsolicitation agreements should always be short-lived.** Confidentiality provisions, by contrast, are often drafted to endure indefinitely.

6) **An assignment of inventions provision may be included.** If you have patents or other inventions to your name, read this language closely and make sure that you are not transferring your rights to the company (without appropriate compensation). A properly drafted agreement will not require that, but it will likely require that any inventions during your employment period belong to the company (so you will want to carve out any exceptions). If you do not have inventions, these provisions may not be relevant, but you nonetheless may be asked to sign them or represent that you have no inventions.

7) **Additional, agreement-specific provisions may apply.** The above factors are not always the only important points in a noncompete or related agreement, so as I mentioned above, make sure to read and assure you understand what you are signing.

Finally, note that future employers may wish to review whatever you have signed, and if the provisions are too onerous (even if unenforceable), they may wish to avoid the risk rather than hiring you and being sued. While they are not signatories, they can nonetheless (in some cases) become embroiled in the proceedings.

## I.      Multiple Offers

If you have multiple offers – lucky you! – this can be a challenging time.

As you are considering your offers, go back to your debrief form or other notes and make sure that you have given deep thought to what is the better choice for the short-term and over your career. For example, a company that pays $5,000 or even $50,000 more per year (depending on your overall compensation) may not be the best choice overall – especially when you consider the portion going to taxes – if it will not allow you room for advancement or limits future mobility.

In some cases, you will need to make a decision about one offer before you receive word from other potential opportunities. As I mentioned above, you can request that a company expedite its decision process, but in some cases this is simply not within their means to do, even if you are a highly desirable candidate. Also, you need to be far enough along in the process (generally having at least two interviews with a target employer under your belt) to credibly do that

If you accept an offer with one company and need to break off the process with others, I would continue to keep in touch with the other companies with which you interviewed. You never know if the job you have accepted will work out – for reasons that only become obvious once you have started there – and it just may be that you wish or need to jump ship quickly. While it does not happen often, it happens often enough to have a safety net whenever possible.

Sometimes, you may receive an offer and go into a panic mode. The offer can come much more quickly than expected, and you still may not have sorted out in your mind whether the job is a good fit for you, whether or not the compensation meets your requirements. An old-fashioned pros and cons list can help, as can conversations with trusted friends and advisors. Your goal is to get to the root of your indecision:

Are you afraid you will hate the job in six months or a few years? What motivated you to apply for the role and have your priorities shifted? Is there an obvious personality conflict with someone who is a key member of management or your new team? Are you concerned that you are too early in the process and may pass up on better opportunities but also don't want to lose this one? How realistic are these concerns?

Notes: _____

**If you are not sure whether to accept a new position, it is almost always a good idea to ask for some time to consider it (at least a few days).**

While there are a handful employers who are truly in a legitimate crunch to get someone with your skills on board, generally a company that treats its employees well starts the process right by giving you time to make this important decision, knowing that if you are pushed to decide, you may make an impulsive and wrong move, which can cost the company (and you) time and money to overcome.

### J.    Counteroffers from Your Current Employer

In most cases, it does not make sense to interview with the hopes that you will receive a counteroffer from your current employer. If compensation is the *only* issue you have with your current job, then in limited cases this could make sense. However, often there are multiple reasons why you may choose to look outside the firm – such as a lack of respect shown or poor communications with your boss – and these often will not be solved through showing "your worth" to third parties. If you receive a counteroffer, subject it to the same scrutiny as any other job offer. Don't let loyalty be your driving force. Six months later (for all you know) your direct supervisor could quit or the company could be out of business.

### K.    Rejections (and How to Recover)

Some candidates bounce back from rejection easily, while others can nurse the wound for months or longer. A "rejection" means that it was not a match – or the interviewer simply got it wrong – and while it can sting, it is in your best interest to move on.

If you are rejected from a firm, you may wish to send a quick, polite note thanking the employer for the opportunity. While you have not received an offer, you may find yourself in the near, medium-term or distant future applying again for another position at the same firm.

### L.    Asking for Feedback

While there is no harm in asking for feedback about your interview, and why you may have been passed up as a candidate, try not to be disappointed if you do not receive a response (instead moving on to other opportunities). Interviewers are often extremely busy and may not have the opportunity to send personalized responses to each individual candidate. In some cases, direct responses to job seekers about why they were not hired may even be discouraged by the interviewer's firm due to public relations or other concerns. Further, an interviewer may not want to offend a job seeker (or open the possibility of a debate or request for reconsideration) in the course of giving negative feedback.

If you do request feedback, you can include it in your thank-you note described at the outset of this chapter. Be ready for whatever feedback may come – whether from the interviewer or a recruiter with whom you are working – accept it graciously and try to use it to improve for the next round of interviews.

## M.   Staying in Touch

As I have mentioned above, if you made a meaningful connection with an individual interviewer or employer but were nonetheless not chosen for the open position, in many cases it makes sense (without going overboard) to continue to follow up. A new position that is more suited to your qualifications or does not (yet) have other candidate submissions may open up any day, and you want to show that you are not only interested in *any new job* but specifically working with that interviewer or employer, as the case may be.

**Notes**

_____

_____

_____

_____

_____

_____

_____

# CONCLUSION

I congratulate you on taking the time to read and complete the exercises in this book, which will propel your professional development at any stage in the interview process.

By now, I hope that you have considered the fundamental interview question enough times, in enough contexts, that you will never forget it. I will refrain from repeating it here.

Remember also, as you continue the interview process, that your own intuition (informed, not raw, intuition) is your best guide, so I encourage you to think of the suggestions here not as rigid rules to be followed but rather as a set of best practices that can and should be tailored to your situation. I have tried at all points to give clear, practical guidance, but there may always be a time that your questions go beyond the answers that are available in this or any other book or reference. For a final pep talk on this front, go back and read the main points in Chapter 4.

Finally, don't forget to take notes in the workbook portions or on additional sheets so that you can refer to them later, whether in a few days, weeks or months from now, when you have your next interview, or years into the future, when you find yourself on the job market again. The best gift that you can give yourself now, beyond the wisdom you have gained from reading this book, is the *gift of momentum*. In other words, if you have your notes at the ready for that inevitable next interview, you will never again have to start from the beginning but instead be two, ten or one hundred steps ahead.

Thank you and best of luck!

*Additional copies of worksheets are available at www.annemariesegal.com, which is simply my first and last name. (Once you are on the site, click on "Worksheets" and choose the applicable form. No passwords or codes are needed.) Feel free to download additional copies at any time, especially if you have run out of room here or are traveling for an interview and do not have space to pack (or forgot to bring) a copy of this book.*

# FINAL NOTES

If you have any other notes that you would like to keep together with your responses in this workbook, and they do not fit in the pages above, please use the space below or tuck in additional pages. Remember, writing clarifies and cements concepts and prepares you for the big sprint – or marathon!

_____

_____

_____

_____

_____

_____

_____

_____

_____

_____

_____

_____

_____

# FURTHER RESOURCES

I am a firm believer in calling on a number of sources and preparing as needed to do your best. Here are some other interview books that may be helpful, each of which approaches the interview process from a different perspective:

*Competency-Based Interviews: How to Master the Tough Interview Style Used by the Fortune 500s,* Robin Kessler (Pompton Plains: Career Press, 2012).

*Interview Like a Boss: The Most Talked-About Book in Corporate America,* by Hans Van Nas (Simon & Schuber, 2014).

*Interview Magic: Job Interview Secrets from America's Career and Life Coach,* Susan Britton Whitcomb (Indianapolis: JIST Works, 2008).

*Knock 'em Dead Job Interview: How to Turn Job Interviews into Job Offers,* Martin Yate CPC (Avon: Adams Media, 2013).

*Top Notch Executive Interviews,* Katherine Hansen, Ph.D. (Franklin Lakes: Career Press, 2010).

**Note:** The above sources are provided for convenience. I feel compelled to disclose that I do not necessarily endorse *all* of the suggestions in the resources above (hence my motivation to write this book). In addition, there are many other helpful books, websites and other media, and you should always consider whether advice matches your specific situation.

Finally, there are additional resources on my blog at www.annemariesegal.com, including copies of many of the workbook portions here. (Please click on "Worksheets.") In addition, I am available to discuss private, one-on-one career and/or interview coaching. Please get in touch with me through my website at www.segalcoaching.com.

# ABOUT THE AUTHOR

 Anne Marie Segal is a career coach, leadership advocate, author and resume writer.

As Founder and Principal of Segal Coaching, she has worked with hundreds of professionals across the U.S. and internationally on career transitions, interview preparation, leadership development and personal branding through individual coaching, writing, workshops and seminars.

With 15 years of experience as a corporate attorney prior to coaching, including 10 years focused on hedge funds and private equity, Anne Marie is a practical, industry-savvy coach and writer. She relishes helping executives, attorneys and other working professionals enhance and communicate their value to themselves and their employers.

Anne Marie holds a J.D. from New York University School of Law, an M.A. in Art History from The University of Chicago and a B.A. in Fine Arts (Photography) from Loyola University of Chicago. She is certified as a Certified Career Management Coach (CCMC) through The Academies and is qualified as a Certified Professional Resume Writer (CPRW).

Anne Marie lives in Stamford, Connecticut with her husband, two children, a cat named Max and a fish named Bob. *Master the Interview* is her first book.

Made in the USA
Middletown, DE
10 January 2018